From the Stone Age to King George III: A History of Weymouth & Its Neighbours

By: A.A. Collier

From the Stone Age to King George III:

A History of Weymouth & Its Neighbours, Volume I

Copyright © 2013 by teacupbooks

Published by teacupbooks

ISBN: 978-0-9576282-0-5

Thank you to Hannah A. Morriss for her excellent technical skills and tremendous patience and to Carol Hunt, author of the Portland Chronicles, for her belief that this community's story should be told and for her encouragement during the long process of researching that story!

Table of contents:

A B C D E F

S O M E R S E T

Sandford Orcas

Trent · Poyntington
Nether · Compton · Oborne
Sherborne
Bradford · Stourton Caun
Abbas · Bishop's Caun
Clifton · Thornford · Holwell
Maybank · Long Burton
Yetminster · King
Leigh · Holnest · Has
Melbury · Stockwood · Wootton Glanville
Osmond
Halstock · West Chelborough · Melbury · Melbury · Hillfield
South Perrott · Corscombe · Sampford · Bubb
East Chelborough · Evershot · Batcombe · Mintern
Forde Abbey · Broadwindsor · Rampisham · Up Cerne · Cerne
Thorncombe · Wraxall · Abbas
Stoke Abbott · Beaminster · Cattistock · Nethe
Piddon · Mapperton · Cerne
Netherbury · Maiden Newton · Sydling
Melplash · Toller Porcorum · St Nicholas · Godmar
Monkton Wyld · Marshwood Vale · Powerstock · Toller Fratrum · Frome Vauchurch
Whitchurch · Eggardon · Frampton
Bradpole · Hill · Wynford · Stratton
Symondsbury · Loders · Compton · Eagle · Cha
Charmouth · Bridport · Abbas · Compton Valence · Stinsf
Chideock · Bothenhampton · Askerswell · Bradford
Lyme Regis · Stanton · Winterborne · Peverell
St Gabriel · Chilcombe · Abbas
Shipton Gorge · Long · Winterborne
Litton Cheney · Bredy · St Martin
Burton Bradstock · Punknowle · Steepleton · Win
Swyre
Portisham · Tatetu
Abbotsbury · Upway · B
Broadway · Prest
Radipole · Sutt
Fleet · Poy
Chesil Beach
Bridge
Wyke Regis · W

E V O N

DORSET

W I L T S H I R E

H A M P S H I R E

Silton
Gillingham
Buckhorn Weston
Motcombe
Kington Magna
East Stour
Shaftesbury
Fifehead Magdalen
West Stour
Todber
Marnhull
Stalbridge
Fontmell Magna
Woodyates
Handley
Pentridge
on St Mary
Sturminster Newton
Farrington
Woodcutts
Gussage St Andrew
Alderholt
ydlinch
Hammoon
Iwerne Minster
Farnham
Wimborne St Giles
Chettle
ock Gaylard
Shillingstone
Shroton
Tarrant Gunville
Gussage St Michael
Cranborne
Neville
Steepleton Iwerne
Tarrant Hinton
Gussage All Saints
Woodlands
keford Fitzpaine
Stourpaine
an Belchalwell
Durweston
Pimperne
More Crichel
Horton
Ibberton
Langton
Chalbury
Wake
Turnworth
Blandford
Witchampton
Woolland
Blandford St Mary
Tarrant Rushton
appowder
Blandford
Charlton Marshall
Tarrant Keynston
Hilton
Winterborne Stickland
Tarrant Crawford
Pamphill
ham Melcombe
Milton Abbas
Spettisbury
Shapwick
Badbury Rings
Wimborne
nthide
Winterborne Whitchurch
Sturminster Marshall
Cheselbourne
Dewlish
Winterborne Kingston
Almer
Corfe Mullen
Canford
West Parley
ehinton
Milborne St Andrew
Winterborne Tomson
Tolpuddle
Bere Regis
Bloxworth
Morden
Lytchett Matravers
wn
elhampton
Turners Puddle
Affpuddle
ncleton
Bryant's Puddle
er Bockhampton
mpston Woodsford
Poole
HESTER
Fordington
Moreton
est Stafford
Lewell
Wareham
Arne
Brownsea
tcombe
West Knighton
Wool
ell
Owermoigne
East Holme
Studland
Poxwell
Winfrith Newburgh
P U R B E C K
n Chaldon
Creech
Church Knowle
Herring
East Lulworth
Corfe
nnstead Lulworth
Tyneham
Steeple
Kingston
Swanage
e
Kimmeridge
Worth Matravers

be Regis

St. Aldhelm's Head

LAND

Her Hea

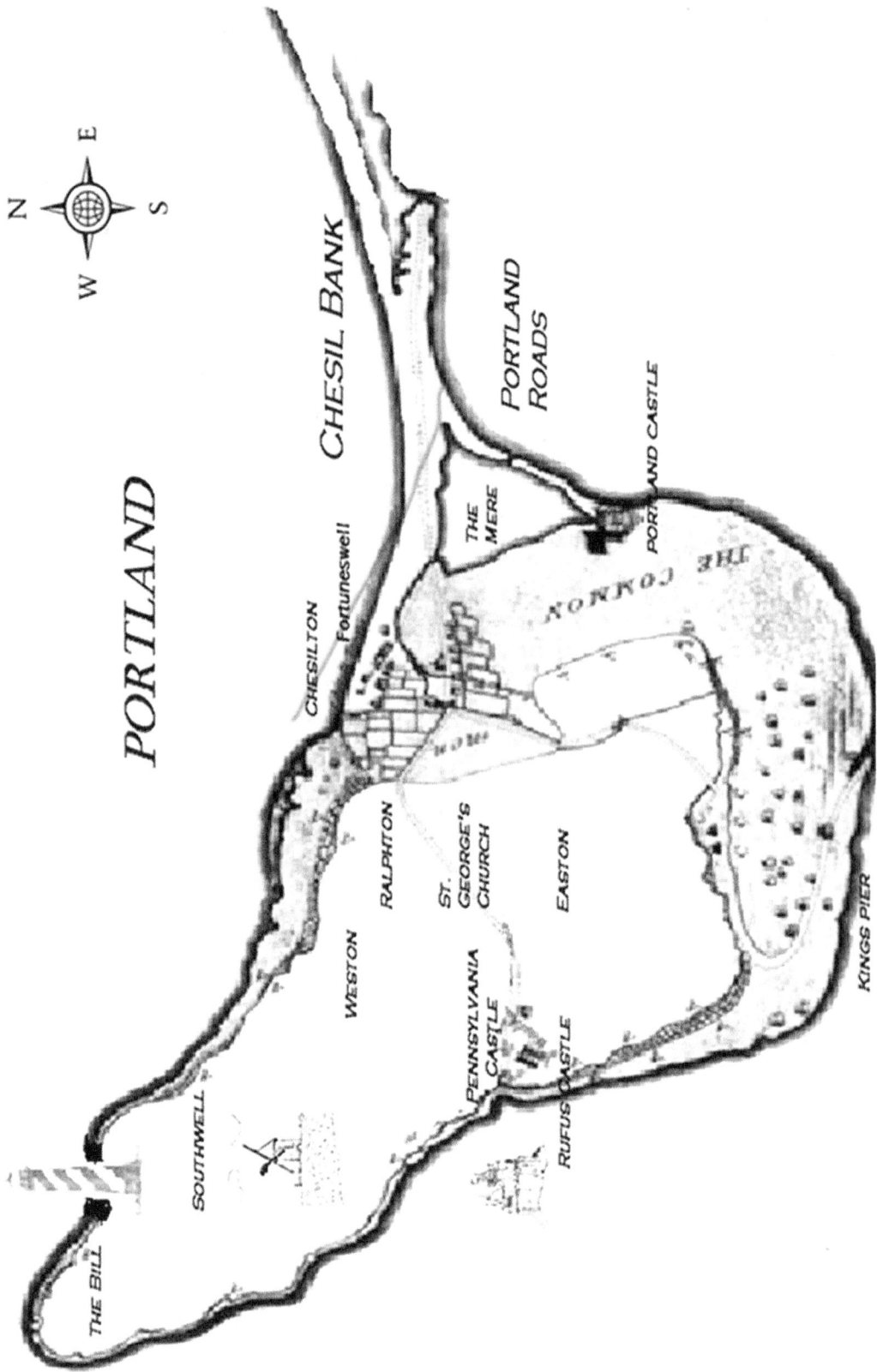

PORTLAND

CHESIL BANK

PORTLAND ROADS

CHESILTON
Fortuneswell

THE MERE

PORTLAND CASTLE

THE COMMON

WESTON

RALPHTON

ST. GEORGE'S CHURCH

EASTON

PENNSYLVANIA CASTLE

RUFUS CASTLE

KINGS PIER

SOUTHWELL

THE BILL

N
E
S
W

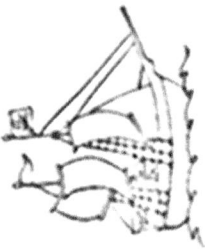

Portland's hill fort

IN THE BEGINNING

Although Africa's first people go back to the early the Stone Age, Great Britain's earliest inhabitants appear to have arrived somewhere between 500,000 and 750,000 years ago. Those people were not settlers, however, they were visitors who came and went according to the weather, an ongoing migration that went on for thousands of years, as the part-time settlers stayed during warm periods and left when extreme cold made it hard to find enough to eat. This easy movement was only possible because Britain was not an island separate from Europe until about 11,000 BC, meaning the early migratory people walked from place to place.

Portland's Culverwell

When we talk about our earliest ancestors, we are not really talking about those early migrant visitors, but the people who came and made this their permanent home; they arrived somewhere between 10,000 and 8000 BC, during the Neolithic era, and though they were also hunter-gatherers, those migrants chose to stay here in Great Britain, following herds of wild animals and other food sources, moving each time they exhausted resources. The Neolithic hunters found a plentiful supply of elk, boar, and deer, for instance, as well as native species of nuts, herbs, fruits, and berries.

Not all Neolithic peoples were in constant movement, however. Some of the best evidence of that is found in Dorset. Portland's Culverwell Neolithic site has been excavated by archeologists, who discovered the site had been inhabited by extended families for many years at a time. They built houses out of local materials, complete with stone floors, making the dwellings both warm and safe. A cooking pit, hearths, tools, and a stone wind break outside of one of the homes were also found, along with piles of shells, evidence that these people enjoyed a year round diet of shell fish. Other artefacts point to those early Portlanders as having some form of spiritual beliefs; they wore "lucky charms" made from the little pebbles with holes in them which could be found along Chesil Beach (Chesil means "hard stone" in Anglo-Saxon). These were hung on a strip of leather and most likely worn around the neck.

The first farmers

The second wave of migration to Great Britain occurred during the Bronze Age in about 2000 BC. This group originated from Southern Europe, but they were farmers not hunter-gatherers. England and much of the rest of Great Britain was heavily forested at this time, requiring those first farmers chop down forests to plant their crops and raise animals: pigs, goats, sheep and cows. By changing the natural environment in this way, the Bronze Age farmers were the first to really interfere with Britain's natural environment, changing it to suit themselves instead of working with it.

It is believed that these prehistoric farmers were so successful in growing their own food and creating stable settlements, by 1400 BC, England probably had a population of at least half a million people. They were also an advanced culture who appreciated decorative items; carvers made beautiful beads from animal bones and hides were sewn to make clothes. Other more exotic goods, some made locally, some coming from other parts of the world, have also been found in local archeological digs. Needles, gold rings, gold plates, bronze daggers, and other decorative objects all demonstrate the talents and diversity of those early people. So though most were farmers, these artefacts demonstrate other skills and trades, with craftsmen producing and trading locally made goods for amber from Baltic tribes and gold from the Irish, meaning that the early Britons were also sailors, miners, traders, goldsmiths, and more.

This trade and the wealth it represented, along with the shifting patterns in human habitation meant a need for defence against invasion, which led to the development of hill forts, many of which are still visible today.

The very last prehistoric, and most important, migration to Great Britain took place at the beginning of the Iron Age; those people came in groups from Europe, and included the Belgae, the Gauls, and most importantly to local history…the *Celts*.

The Dur-o-tree-gays

Dorset's Iron Age Celtic people were called the Durotriges (pronounced *dur-o-tree-gays*) which means *water dwellers*, a reference to the fact that the earliest migrants lived along side or very near the local waters. The Celts are probably best known for their hill fortresses, those they inherited from earlier people and improved on and those they built themselves, both inland and along the Dorset coast. These were necessary for defence against the last of the other tribes arriving in Great Britain before the Roman conquest in the first century AD. Tribes like the Belgae, coming from what is now Belgium, continued to trickle in and of course there was always the threat from marauders and bands of thieves who were not tied to community or tribe.

The hill forts acted as a kind of route through the county, probably intended as shelters for those who lived and travelled between them; the Durotriges' forts were so large, requiring a big labour force to build them, they are an indication that the Celts had slaves who did much of the manual labour and more than likely used prisoners of war to help build the huge defences.

Dorset hill fortresses, often referred to as castles, included: Abbotsbury, Hod Hill, Hambleton Hill, Badbury Rings, Eggardon Hill, the Nothe, Verne Hill, Flowers's Barrow Camp, and Chalbury Hill. And the most impressive hill fort, built around 2000 BC and expanded over time, was Maiden Castle, which stands just outside of Dorchester.

Durgotrige girls would have been called Aberfa, Ceri, Bridget, Jestine, Ffanci, Ebrill, Isode, or Ysbail. Popular boys' names included Afal, Conyn, Gwyr, Newlin, Steffan, Myrlyn, Ysberin, and Rhett. Some of these are familiar today.

Maiden Castle was home to the local king because Dorchester was the Durgotriges' tribal centre. When the Romans invaded the area, they called the town Durnovaria, which means "small stones of the water" probably because of the small stones the Celts collected along the coast and used to defend themselves. They were such an important part of the Celt's system of defence that large mounds of them were stored within the fortress walls.

This castle, or fortification, is the finest example of an Iron Age fort in the entire country and covers over 47 acres, the largest of its type not just in England but in Europe. It is so vast, it could have housed at least 4000 people during a siege, designed to protect the local clans at times of fear of attack from invaders.

Some archaeologists and historians have postulated that the Durgotriges lived in their forts, using them as fortified villages, but that is not the case. The local Celts were busy people who worked family farms, travelled on business, fished, and traded amongst themselves. During times of peace, they lived together in *clans*, meaning *children*. The clan was a small group based on family ties, each one connected to another through tribal ancestry. It was the tribal leaders who lived at least part time within the fortress. They in turn had their own warriors, whose job it was to protect the leaders and to maintain a communication system that helped keep watch for possible invasion; whenever there was a threat from outside, the warriors let as many of the clans know as possible and those small groups made their way to the safety of the castle. During the Middle Ages, castles were still used for this purpose.

Although the hill fort was essentially meant for defence, they were hives of activity during peace time; maintenance, extensions, and improvements meant a constant stream of people coming and going. And of course, as many of the hill forts were also the residences of the Celtic kings, they would have been the centres of official business.

The Celtic castle was a real feat of ancient engineering; the interior included living space, water and food storage areas, long vertical shafts so that valuables could be hidden away in case of marauders, and of course, plenty of storage for weapons. But it is perhaps the entrance that reflects the remarkable talent of the Celtic engineers. Referred to as "chicane entrances," they were designed to slow down invaders who rushed into the covered entrance and down the corridor, only to find that there was a sharp turn up ahead; a sort of Z shaped hallway. This helped the Celtic warriors lay in wait for anyone who breached the entrance during times of siege, hopefully trapping the first entrants and preventing anyone else from entering.

When it was peaceful, people came and went via foot or travelled in wagons and chariots; in the case of very large forts like Maiden Castle, they drove over a bridge that spanned the ditches surrounding the fort; the ditches were dug in order to make it difficult for invaders to get into the fort "around the back." And during war time, the entrance had to be both closable and defensible, which required a large, lockable gate.

Early warfare tactics addressed the need to get through those gates with something called 'stoning and firing.' This phrase literally describes just how an enemy raiding party would approach its target; a small group of warriors were sent up to the gate, where they would sling stones at the defending warriors who stood on the ramparts above the entry and around the fort itself. If the raiding party were successful in moving forward, this allowed a couple of the men to get right up to the gate and set it on fire.

Once the gate burned down, the waiting raiders could run up to and enter the fort and all would probably be lost to its inhabitants. There is evidence at some of the Dorset hill forts that wooden gates were burned down, replaced, and then, burned down again; Badbury Rings is one of those, where several layers of burned entrance gates have been discovered.

CHALBURY CAMP DORSET SITE D HUT CIRCLE Nº 8

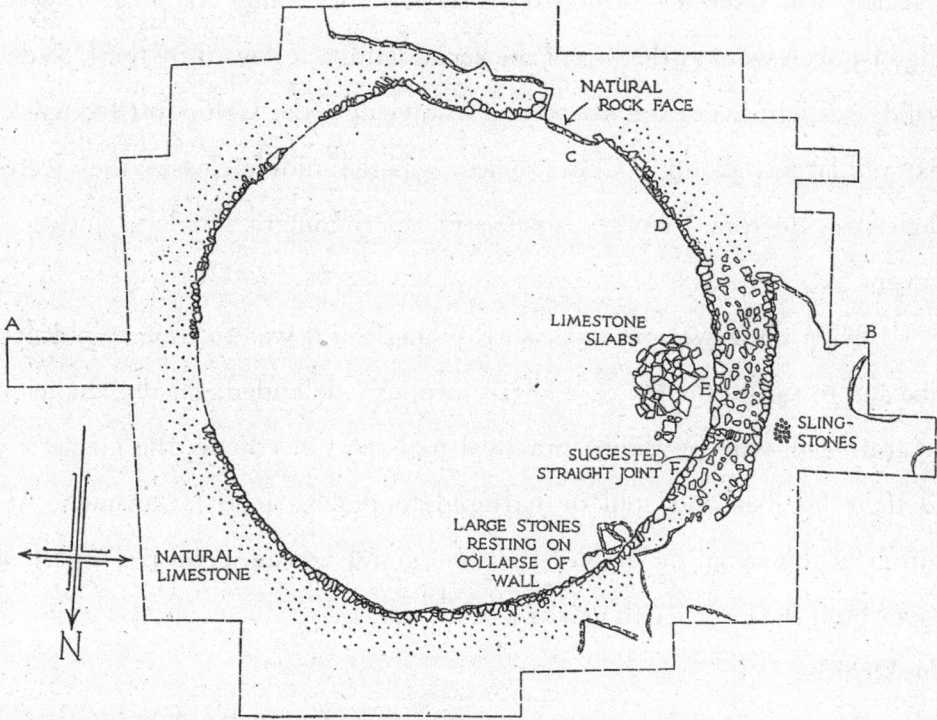

NATURAL
ROCK FACE

C

D

LIMESTONE
SLABS

B

E

SLING-
STONES

SUGGESTED
STRAIGHT JOINT F

A

LARGE STONES
RESTING ON
COLLAPSE OF
WALL

NATURAL
LIMESTONE

N

SECTION A–B

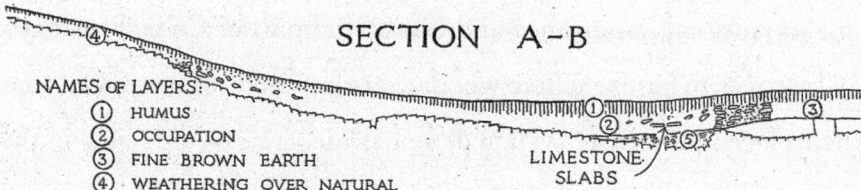

NAMES OF LAYERS:
1. HUMUS
2. OCCUPATION
3. FINE BROWN EARTH
4. WEATHERING OVER NATURAL
5. QUARRY DEBRIS

LIMESTONE
SLABS

NOTE: *Illustrated finds from all layers Nos. 19–42, 50–56.*

SCALE OF FEET
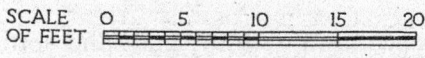
0   5   10   15   20

SCALE OF METRES
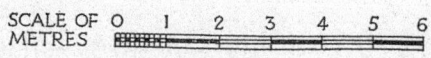
0   1   2   3   4   5   6

ELEVATION C–D

SCALE OF FEET
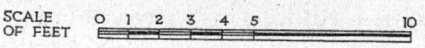
0 1 2 3 4 5   10

ELEVATION E–F

SUGGESTED STRAIGHT
JOINT

SCALE OF METRES
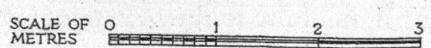
0   1   2   3

Chalbury's Sling Stones

7

Being a Celt...

Celtic society was based on a caste system, in which a person's position in society was fixed according to profession and family standing. The ruling king or queen were at the top of the social ladder, followed by the Druids and Druidesses who were the keepers of knowledge, the Celtic intellectuals. The next and largest group in Celtic society was the middle classes; they were the magicians, doctors, bards, astrologers, astronomers, traders, judges and lawyers.

Then there were the warriors, whose job it was to train to protect the tribe and to assure the fortresses were properly defended. Finally, the menials, the craftsmen who produced practical tools and of course, the farmers, who fed their families and sold or bartered food with fellow clansmen. At the bottom of the social order were prisoners and hostages, people whose slave labour built the large earth works.

The Druids

The word Druid is thought to mean "oak knowledge." The oak was revered for its spiritual importance and was a vital part of Celtic life; they planted oak groves to assure whole woods were devoted to the special tree. And as their place in the caste system demonstrates, the Druids' role in the class structure of the Celts was not as a separate group, they were the spiritual leaders of their people, officiating at all religious events, and regulating public and private ceremonies that required intervention with the gods and spirits. The Druids were also the keepers of all knowledge and part of their job was to keep that knowledge sacred; this meant that they did not keep written records. Instead, they memorized everything that was considered important, passing it on orally to the next generation of Druids. This is why there are no written records produced by the Celts themselves, making the objects and fortresses they left behind terribly important in helping to tell their story.

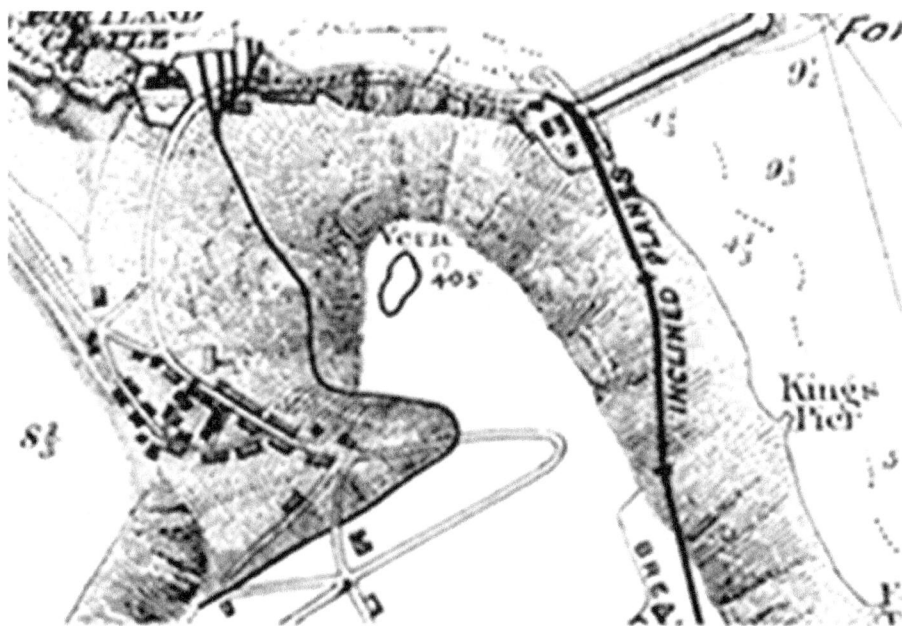

1857 Sketch of Portland's Fort

Dorset's Gibraltar

Probably the most visible of the ancient hill forts of Dorset was Portland's. Although it is believed there was a late Palaeolithic settlement on the Verne, a Brittonic word for *alder grove*, (where a stone henge stood until the latter half of the 19th century) as long ago as 10,000 BC, a significant hill fort had been constructed on that site by 2000 BC; the Isle was a recognised trading port as long ago as the early Bronze Age. Often referred to as an "earthworks" by early chroniclers of Portland geography, the fort was described as a large enclosure *'protected by a double rampart and corresponding ditches, while the area bore the appearance of having peculiar nature of the ground, and at a small outlay of labour, a double escarpment, forming as if it were two terraces, was made, materially increasing the strength of the camp. These escarpments extended beyond the camp, following the curvature of the valley some few hundred yards'*...Dorset antiquary Charles Warne, 1872.

Almost 200 years prior to Warne's description, a 17th century

45

46

47

49

48

50

51

52

53

54

55

56

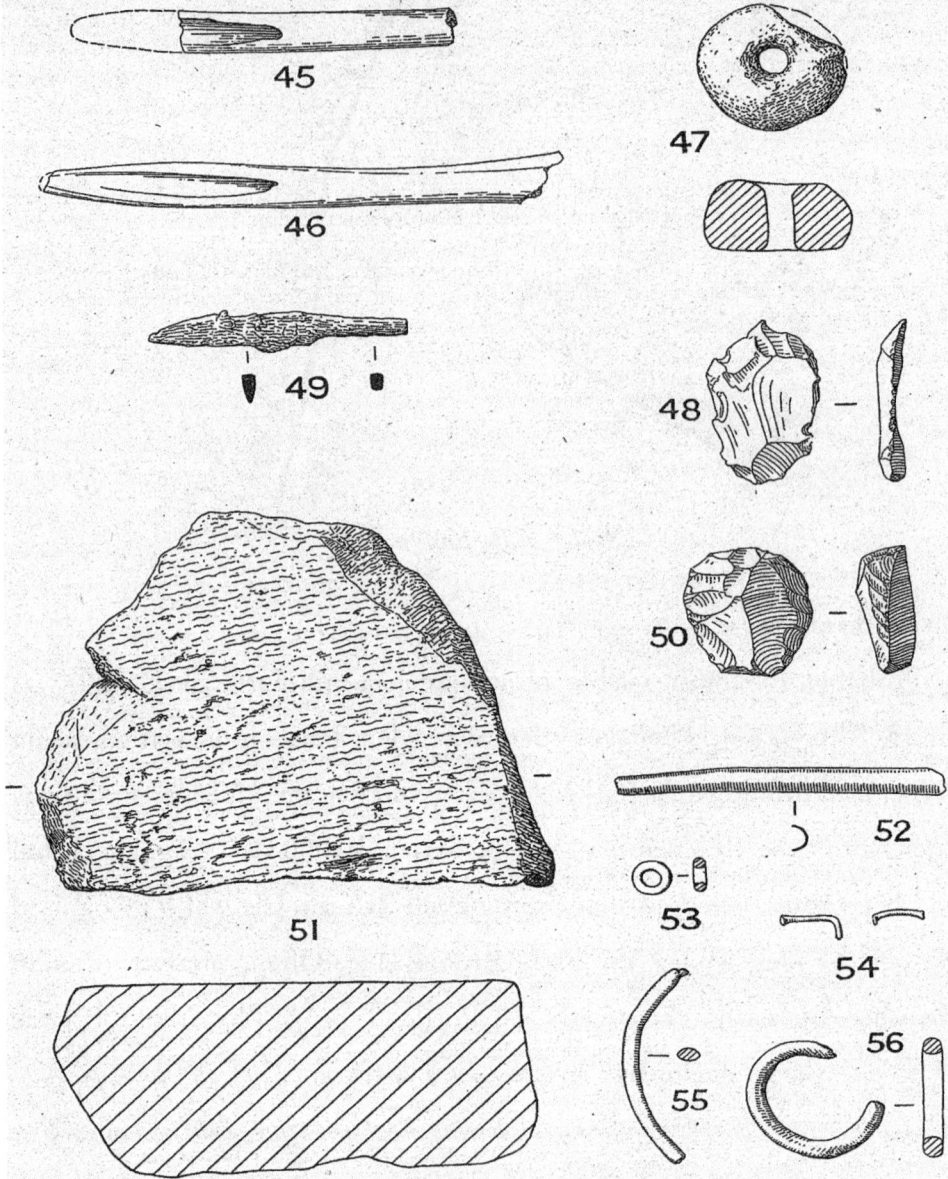

FIG. 8. Small finds. Nos. 45–52 (½). Nos. 53–56 (¼).

Finds From Chalbury Hill Fort

antiquarian, John Aubrey, described a pre-Roman 'double-worked camp,' and the 18th century Dorset topographer John Hutchins wrote about an 'entrenched camp' that was 'ancient British,' meaning Celtic in origin, found at the top of Portland.

The hill fort was readily visible until the military destroyed it by building, in the 1860s, the facility that stands there today, but archaeologists, before the building excavations ruined the ancient fort, did identify the original layout and boundaries of Portland's ancient "castle." Two similar forts built around the same period in Weymouth sat at either end of the modern boundaries of the town; Chalbury Hill fort is still clearly visible, but the Nothe's fort was destroyed when a military facility was built in the late 19th century.

Celtic villages...

Celtic Roundhouse

Many of the Celts of Dorset lived on their own farms, others in small hamlets, which is probably how some of the towns and villages of Dorset, to include Dorchester, Melcombe Regis, Wyke Regis, Portesham, Upwey, Preston, Weymouth and Portland began.

Their homes were made from wood and thatch, a water reed which was plentiful all along the Fleet, around the rivers, and in the bogs of Weymouth; like the earlier homes found on Portland, their foundations were often made of local stone which made them solid and helped to keep them warm in the winter. These homes are called roundhouses because they were literally built in a circular design.

Inside some of the homes, there were sleeping quarters with raised wooden bed frames, feather or hay mattresses, and animal skins and woollen blankets for warmth. During cold weather, fires fuelled with dried animal dung and logs kept the house snug. There was also a cooking and eating area, where the simple diet of the Celts was prepared. They raised their own meat and grains, and supplemented their diets with fish and other wild foods still found in the countryside surrounding Weymouth and Portland today: wild garlic, sorrel, herbs, sloes, and bilberries.

The homes also had a spot set aside for the family loom, used to weave sheep's wool; this provided clothing and blankets, and was made from wood and local stone. It appears that children also had their own small spaces where they could play games similar to modern board games. Outside they could also practice slinging rocks from leather slings, a sort of apprenticeship in learning how to defend themselves, their families and their communities.

The local Celts met in central locations to trade in pottery, tin, jewellery, salt, cows, hides, gold, wool, skins, grain, and other goods. Fellow tribesmen, those who lived in places like Poole, Wareham, and further afield in Devon, Wiltshire and Somerset, exchanged their goods with the locals. Celts from Poole were probably the most successful, as the pottery made from clay from Poole Harbour was highly prized. Iron Age people used a wide variety of clay pots to eat and drink from, store grains and seeds in, and to collect fresh water in, which made pottery a valuable commodity.

They also traded with outside tribes, travelling as far away as Europe to buy and sell practical and luxury goods. Hengistbury Head, where there was a significant hill fortress, is thought to have been the Iron Age's busiest southern port, where many of the goods from Europe arrived, but Weymouth and Portland were also centres of trade. During the Bronze Age, Portlanders traded with Gaul, evidenced by the Amorica-style pottery found around the island. It was also an important supplier of chert, a stone similar to flint, which was traded all over Southern England during the same era. Later, salt works from the base of the island and running up Chesil Bank supplied another valuable trade item throughout the Iron Age.

Spiritual Stones

Celtic sites of worship were built near each of the local centres of trade and commerce, some of them inherited from earlier tribes. Here people gathered to celebrate the different seasons and to venerate their gods, which included making sacrifices to those gods. Animals played a big part in Celtic religion and the most important were the horse and the bull.

> Kings and Queens - Unlike later societies, Celts did not practice primogeniture, which means a king passed his kingship onto his son; they believed instead that a king had to be a capable leader in order to deserve the job. That was true of Queens, too. England's most famous Celtic leader was Queen Boadicea, who led her army against the Romans, destroying most of London in the process.

When a new king was appointed, a bull was sacrificed and he ate the meat and drank a broth made from its blood. They believed that because the bull was a powerful, virile animal, those traits would be passed on to the king.

The horse was at least as commonly sacrificed as the bull; horse bones have been found at most of the henges, spiritual centres created by placing large stones in a circular pattern, across Great Britain. It is not surprising then that one of the most important Celtic deities was the horse-goddess Epona. The Durotriges even had a horse figure on some of their coins.

Other animal bones, to include human remains, have also been found at important spiritual centres throughout Dorset; it has been rumoured for over a thousand years that the Celtic Druids practiced human sacrifice at these sites. Both animal and human bones were found during the excavation of the local Chalbury Hill fort.

Although there is little left of the local henges, there are remnants of wooden henges and large Saracen stonge henges scattered in farmer's fields around the country; they had great spiritual significance throughout the county. These include Portesham's Hellstone and the Grey Mare and Her Colts, as well as Mount Pleasant and Maumbury Rings in and near Dorchester, Nice Stones near Winterbourne Abbas, Kingston Russell near Little Bredy, and though no longer visible, there was a sizeable henge on the Verne on Portland. And not too far from Dorset, Stonehenge in Somerset, which was also part of the Durotriges territory, remains standing and is a fantastic example of this kind of place of worship.

Language and money…

The Celtic tribes, to include the Durotriges, spoke Brittonic, sometimes spelled Brythonic, which had its roots in ancient India. The modern names used to refer to both this country and its people come directly from that ancient language: "Britain" and "British" are derived from Brittonic.

Philologists have found that there are other Celtic words still in use today: hubbub, dad, bucket, peat, crock, noggin, gob and nook all meant the same thing to the Celts as they do to us, except that the slang of today was the "proper" term of the past. They also put their babies in *cradles*, eight *rashers* of bacon, drank *beer*, cleaned with *mops*, and cooked on *gridirons*. They made *baskets* and kept *geese*, farmed with *harrows* on their *arable* land, and *harvested* their crops. Their pots were made in *kilns*. Their warriors used *claymores* and their sailors were experts in navigating their *coracles*. Celtic chieftains were buried in *barrows* and the rain made *puddles*, which they *skipped* over.

There are also Celtic words still used as place names. Locally, there is

Portesham's Hellstone "henge"

Frome, as in the River Frome, a word which means "fine, fair and brisk." Then there is Owermoigne, a small village outside of Weymouth, whose name is Brittonic for "wind gap." Some have explained that word's etymology differently, however. There are locals who believe that the original name of the Saxon village on this site was Ogre which later became Oweres. The owners of the land in and near the village during the Middle Ages were the Le Moignes. Over time, the two names came together to create "Overmoigne." Perhaps the philologist's explanation for the Brittonic name and meaning actually explains where both the Saxon village and a local family got their names, not the other way around.

Celtic Coins from the collection of Thomas Herbert, Eighth Earl of Pembroke (1656 – 1733), found in Portland Quarries and the Verne

Although it is the Romans who are credited with minting the first coins in Great Britain, it was actually the Durotriges who introduced this practice; they were ahead of their time in using coinage instead of barter for goods and services. Their coinage was made from various metals, to include gold, and is further evidence of what brilliant metal smiths the Celts were. And they did not just make coins and other practical items like knives, needles, daggers, and horse harnesses. At Maiden Castle, bracelets, earrings, rings, hair ornaments and broaches have been found and at Jordan Hill in Preston, archaeologists have uncovered other decorative items demonstrating excellent craftsmanship to include glass bead jewellery, horse shoes and drinking cups made from antlers.

The Nothe's Ancient Hill Fort

"ABOUT MATTERS BRITISH"

About matters British I understand from your letters that there is nothing there about which we should either tremble or rejoice. Cicero, Roman philosopher and statesman, 1st Century AD

The prehistoric era came to an abrupt end when the Romans conquered England in 43 AD. The Emperor Julius Caesar had visited ten years earlier and he clearly disagreed with Cicero, who believed there was nothing here to "tremble or rejoice about." In fact, the trip left Caesar convinced that Great Britain would be an excellent addition to his Empire. He also wanted to gain the glory of a victory beyond the "Great Ocean," which is what the Romans called the English Channel, and he was convinced that Britain was rich in silver and other precious metals he could exploit.

Caesar's first expedition in 55 BC, however, was not well thought out;

with only two legions of soldiers, he failed to do much more than force his way ashore at Deal to win a token victory that impressed the senate in Rome more than it did the British tribes, who fought the Romans off without too much bother. In 54 BC, Caesar tried again, this time with five legions, but still, he went back to Gaul without anything to show for his efforts, complaining in a letter to Cicero that indeed he had been correct, there was no silver or booty to be found in Britain after all.

Even though Caesar's military adventurism had not really achieved very much for the Roman Empire, the desire did not die with Caesar; when Claudius became emperor he used the same excuse as Caesar: he wanted a victory "across the Great Ocean" to bring glory to his reign. Claudius became emperor in a palace coup and needed the prestige of military conquest to consolidate his hold on power. In AD 43, he sent four legions to Britain, one of those led by General Vespasian, who became emperor some years after the invasion. He entered at Richborough in Kent, once a busy port and inhabited by a tribe called the Atrebetes. Their king had no allegiance to other British tribes and was eager to be friends with the Romans so he made no attempt to stop the invasion.

From there, Vespasian marched his army to Dorset, where the Durotriges resisted from their fortifications at Hod Hill, Hambleton Hill, Badbury Rings, and Maiden Castle, eventually making their way to the Weymouth and Portland forts.

Recognising the importance of Maiden Castle, the Romans stormed its ramparts and cut down the brave Celtic warriors as they tried to defend their own territory. The Castle did have those *chicane entrances*, cleverly designed entries that slowed down invaders, but for all their ingenuity, the Celts did not stand a chance against the Roman's "secret weapon."

Much of the Roman success is credited to a brutal weapon they used against the Durotriges: the *ballista bolt*. This was a large mechanically hurled spear, shot directly over the walls of the forts and into the roundhouses; it was launched from a wooden and iron catapult which could shoot a "bolt" from quite a distance but still hit its target. The primary weapons of the Celts, on the other hand, were thousands of stones collected from Chesil Beach and shot from sling shots, along with spears and knives, not enough against such a brutal and well prepared enemy.

The Ballista Bolt

Although the Romans lost hundreds of soldiers - many of whom are buried in graves at Maiden Castle - they succeeded which meant they now controlled the Durotriges and their lands.

Burial and afterlife

The graves of some of the Celts who fought against the Romans have been excavated by archaeologists, revealing just how the Durotriges treated their war dead; the fallen soldiers were buried both in small groups and individually, their bodies placed in a

Durotriges Grave

sort of circular manner, rather than laid straight out into the grave or coffin; this ritual was unique to them. They also buried their dead, those who had not fallen in battle, in deep shafts called vaults, located at sites of worship, such as Jordan Hill. This was unique to the Durotriges; other Iron Age people cremated the remains of their dead, rather than burying the bodies.

Jordan's Hill – The word Jordan probably comes from the Celtic term "Dwrdun," which means "the hill by the water."

The wealthy Durotriges had similar death rituals to the Ancient Egyptians, who were buried with everything they thought they would need in the afterlife as well as those things they most cherished. The Celts did the same: pottery, glassware, spears, even games have been uncovered in the chambers of local grave sites. The local ruling classes were buried in mounds called barrows, which were always near a fort or henge. These earth structures have walls and tombs made of solid oak. The bodies of the leaders were placed in the tombs and surrounded by their belongings, which could include chariots, wagons, personal ornaments, utensils, and even food and drink. They did this to make sure their kings and other important people were prepared for the *Otherworld*. There are many barrows still visible in the

Weymouth area, to include near Chalbury Fort and the Bincombe Bumps, a series of barrows above the tiny village of Bincombe.

Early multiculturalism

Although the Romans killed many Durotriges and other Britons as they conquered the island, the majority of the Celts survived the invasion, becoming what historians refer to as the "Romano-Britons." Those who cooperated and did not take up arms were not attacked by the army as it marched through England, living much as they had before, except under the rule of the Romans. Others escaped to Brittany, another word derived from the Celts' native language Brittonic, and a few even moved north west, probably to Cornwall.

The Romans were always brutal as they invaded new lands, but once they had conquered a territory and its people, it was Roman policy to absorb those people rather than eliminate them. Some locals traded with and lived near or even next to the Roman soldiers, traders, and bureaucrats who arrived with the army. Especially given the policy of encouraging their soldiers to intermarry with the locals they had conquered, this era provides an example of how diverse British society was becoming, something that would continue to present day. There is no such thing as "pure" British blood, it is a nation shaped by many different peoples, languages, and cultures coming together as one, sometimes peacefully, sometimes through force, all of which is reflected in the local story.

The Durotriges were not treated as a separate tribe by the Romans; *all* the British natives conquered by the Romans were treated "the same" and were referred to as Brittones, or when they were unhappy with them, Brittunculi, which can be translated as either "little Brits" or "wretched Brits." Interestingly, though, many of the Roman soldiers who came here to conquer and those who stayed were not actually Romans in the sense that few of them were born in Italy. Most of them were from Batavia and Tunria, modern

Holland and Belgium, which meant that they may have shared a common origin with the *Brittones*.

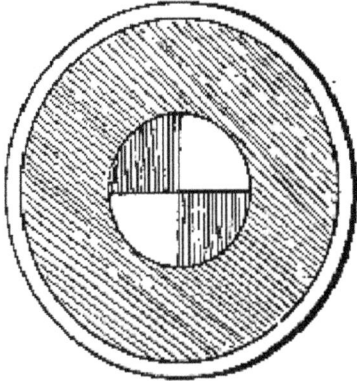

Those areas of Europe had been conquered shortly before the invasion of Britain and it was Roman policy to enlist local men of newly conquered territory into their army. They believed military service led "new Romans" to feel they had an allegiance to the empire, meaning they would be loyal to it. True to this philosophy, only fifty years after they were conquered, British men, some from Dorset, were legionnaires in the Roman army: the "ala Britannica" units served in Pannonia, today's Austria and Hungary.

Shield of a Brittanci Soldier

Wine, garum and dormice?

Much of daily life in Dorset would not have changed very much under Roman rule; the Celts continued to farm, raise livestock, trade, and produce the goods they wanted and needed for their everyday lives, but the new rulers did introduce some uniquely Roman ideas, practices, and entertainments. Durnovaria, today's Dorchester ("Dur" meaning water in Brittonic and chester from the Latin castra, meaning camp), was expanded to serve as the administrative centre from which the Romans ruled the rest of Dorset; they built an aqueduct, a Roman invention designed to bring clean drinking water to places that did not have natural springs; public baths where everyone was welcome to bathe; shops specialising in a wide variety of goods; and amphitheaters for public entertainments.

Instead of drinking beer, the Celt's favourite, many would have adopted the Roman's favourite drink, wine, which was brought directly from Italy to Weymouth harbour and sold by wine merchants throughout Dorset.

Wine became so popular that by the Middle Ages, there were vineyards scattered around the Dorset countryside.

Although it is not clear whether the Celts also liked the Roman's favourite sauce, there is no doubt it would have been available. A kind of ancient ketchup called Garum, this smelly concoction was made from locally caught fermented fish and generously poured over popular dishes like lentil stew and roasted meat, even their very favourite meal of all: stuffed dormouse.

Dorchester's Roman Amphitheater

Settled Romans

There were Roman settlements all over Dorset, to include Dorchester, Weymouth, Portland and their surrounding areas. Unfortunately, Saxon and later Medieval builders used the stone from the extensive Roman structures in their own buildings, which means there are not as many architectural examples from that era of local history as there might otherwise be. There are still, though, some interesting sites that help tell the story.

What were they called? Romano-Britons often combined Celtic with Latin names. For instance, a common first name for a boy in Rome was Julius, so Romano-British parents might have named their son Julius Myrlyn; a popular Roman girl's name was Blanda, so a girl could have been called Blanda Jesstin. This practice may be the origin of the modern "middle name."

At Preston there is a visible ruin of a Roman temple on Jordan Hill, a settlement referred to by the Romans as Clavinio, built over the earlier Celtic development sometime in the 4th or 5th century; a large cache' of gold coins was found above Bowleaze Cove, not far from the temple, indicating just how important that site must have been. Trade to and from that spot would have been made possible by the galleys and locally made dugout canoes that plied local waters. One of the four main roads built by the Romans ran right through Preston, with the southern road going from the hub, located in Dorchester, to Preston and on to Radipole. That small village was also very important because of its strategic location; at that time, boats could navigate their way from the harbour, up the River Wey, and in to Radipole's small port. It was an ideal location for both river transport and its connection to the Roman turnpike going to Dorchester.

It is thought that though the Jordan Hill was primarily a place of worship, it might also have been located right on that part of the coast because it was an ideal look out for ships. With its small protected bay just below the cliffs where a watch may have been kept for this purpose, there is little doubt that this is exactly why the Romans continued to occupy and expand their presence there.

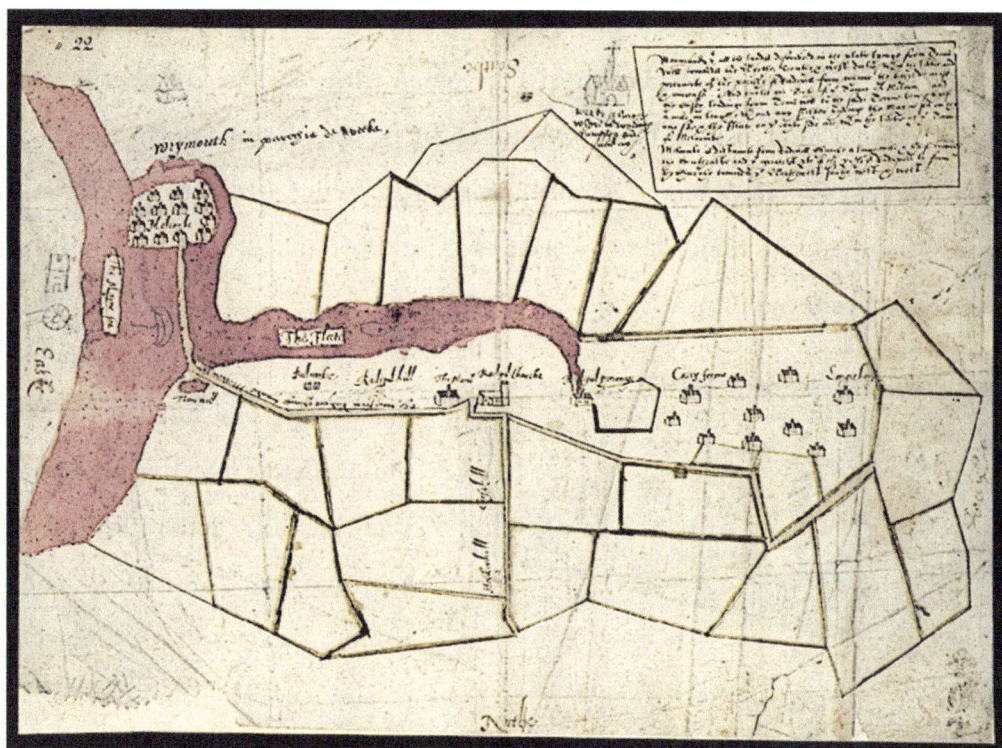

Radipole Map

There are other important Roman roads that can still be found throughout Dorset. All were designed to provide the fastest route from one place to another. The Old Road coming up through Fortuneswell on Portland illustrates perfectly the Roman philosophy when it came to building roads: go "straight." It is incredibly steep and would have been very challenging for men and animals to ascend, but it provided a direct route for locals as they travelled to the top of the Isle and back. The Romans also laid the ground work for the modern villages of Portland by tapping into the natural water sources there: Fortuneswell, Southwell, and Wakeham all had natural springs over which the Romans built wells.

The most important Roman legacy to local history though has to be quarrying. Because of Portland's location, the stone from its cliff edges could be chipped off and pushed into the sea, where it was loaded on to barges. Some of these were towed across the harbour, up the River Wey, and in to

Radipole's port. From there the giant Portland stones were loaded on to wagons and sent via the Ridgeway (the Roman turnpike) to Dorchester and beyond. Other loads would have been taken by boat to various ports along the coast. Even the sarcophagi - stone coffins - in which Romans who could afford them buried their dead, were made of Portland stone; hundreds of those have been found locally.

Roman Sarcophagi

The knowledge of quarrying was not lost when the Romans left England, but was passed, generation after generation, meaning that Rome's legacy to local industry is the success quarrying has enjoyed for almost 2000 years, up to the present day.

Although the Romans did have a tremendous impact on the physical nature, customs, and even personal eating and drinking habits of Dorset and its people, perhaps the greatest change their rule brought to the British Celtic, now the Romano-British, way of life was how and who they worshipped. Their religion was changed forever with the arrival of the Romans.

Goddesses, gods, and the Pantheon

Jordan Temple in Preston had been a site of worship since at least the Bronze Age, and many artefacts have been found there from both the Bronze and the Iron Ages. There was also a round temple in Maiden Castle where the Durgotriges worshipped their local gods and all the other hill forts in the area had small temples dedicated to the indigenous cults.

Although the Celts of England shared common religious practices, each tribe had its own gods and its own way of worshipping those deities. There is not a great deal of information available about the local gods, but the presence of animal and bird bones is an indication that they worshipped particular local species. It is also true that all Celtic, and earlier peoples, believed that rivers, trees, hills, and for those who lived on or near the coasts, fish and the sea, had spiritual meaning; each one was inhabited by spirits. Bathing was also an important ritual in Celtic spiritual life and that was because it was part of the worship of water, which was thought to cleanse the spirit as well as the body.

Celtic gods and goddesses were celebrated not just at temples, but were also represented at the local henges. They included Barinthus, the sea god; Belatucadros, the god of war; and the goddesses of hunting and rivers, Cocidius and Coventina, would have been important to those living along and near the Rivers Frome and Wey.

Preston's Jordan Hill and its temple are a good example of how places of worship were often passed on to or shared with other "faiths." It was held sacred by the Celts and then adopted by the Romans soon after they invaded, a tactic they used throughout their empire. The Romans did this because they were very open-minded about the religious practices of the people they conquered; as long as the Celts were willing to accept Roman gods and goddesses, Roman rulers were happy to include the Celtic deities into their "pantheon," the big group of gods the Romans worshipped. But it is clear that just as the Celts, especially those who lived in towns, began to adopt Roman practices like going to the public baths and wearing togas, their gods began to blend in with the Roman gods, losing their unique qualities.

The Celtic god Lugus, who was associated with wealth, for instance, melded in to Mercury, the Roman god of trade and profit, with Lugus losing his uniquely Celtic qualities. It is also clear that the Celts stopped building places of worship dedicated to their gods and goddesses, and ceased to celebrate their uniquely Celtic holidays. Part of this had to do with the fact that though the Romans were tolerant, the Romano-British did occasionally attempt rebellion, and it was the cult priests who were responsible for trying to organise those overthrows. Roman rulers, in response to those attempts, were not as tolerant of British religious practices as they were with those of peoples who did not try to rebel.

Weymouth Bay

When the Empire crumbled...

During their 400 years of occupation, the Romans were never able to conquer and control all of England, Wales or Scotland; they gave up trying when the rest of their empire began to crumble in the 4th century AD and abandoned Great Britain all together in the beginning of the 5th century, about 410 AD. This decision was made for two reasons: the Romans were struggling to maintain control of the rest of their huge empire as Germanic tribes were invading not only large parts of Europe, but Rome itself, and because tribes from Europe and Scandinavia were conducting more and more raids both along the English coast and further inland, making life difficult for both the

Roman military and the British people.

By 425 AD, Britain was alone, with no central government; the Roman army had left and the Roman Empire itself had crumbled. Many cities and towns throughout Europe and Great Britain were abandoned, with their inhabitants returning to live off the land, some working on the larger farms - called manses - where they sought work and protection from the land owners. This is the beginning of a historical phenomenon called "feudalism," when central government no longer existed and people lived in small groups, in some ways similar to the earlier tribal lifestyle of the Durotriges, but without the tribal ties and cultural traditions they had once enjoyed. It was a painful era, when few written records, something the Romans had been diligent in maintaining, were kept. Britons were simply trying to "survive." This era has for centuries been referred to as "The Dark Ages," dark both because of the lack of a written record of what was happening as well as because there was no central leadership.

A veiw of Weymouth Bay

THE NEXT MIGRATION

When the Roman army exited to help defend the city of Rome just before its fall, it left Britons defenceless against the invasion. From 450 - 750 AD, Danish Vikings, along with European tribes called Angles, Saxons, and Jutes from what is now northern Germany and northern Holland, rowed across the North Sea in wooden boats, landing on British shores, often terrorising the native British. Some of the newcomers were attracted to what they assumed was a wealthy place because it had been a part of the Roman empire, raiding the English of anything they could find of value, but others were hoping to find a new place to live, similar to the movement of tribes millennia before. Some of these groups arrived with farm animals, tools, and weapons; because there were so many of the new immigrants, they eventually became the majority across the country, although they never overcame all of the Celtic peoples in Cornwall, Wales, or Scotland.

As the Angles settled in various parts of England, they do not seem to have interacted with the Britons, choosing to live separately instead, but the larger group, the Saxons, became quite powerful as their population spread out. They did not, however, adopt the Brittonic language, maintaining instead their own Germanic dialects. It is these factors which influenced how and what we speak today; although it has preserved a little bit of the ancient tongue, modern English is derived from German. Even the word *England* means "land of the Angles," and *Anglo-Saxon* is a modern reference to the heritage of the English people.

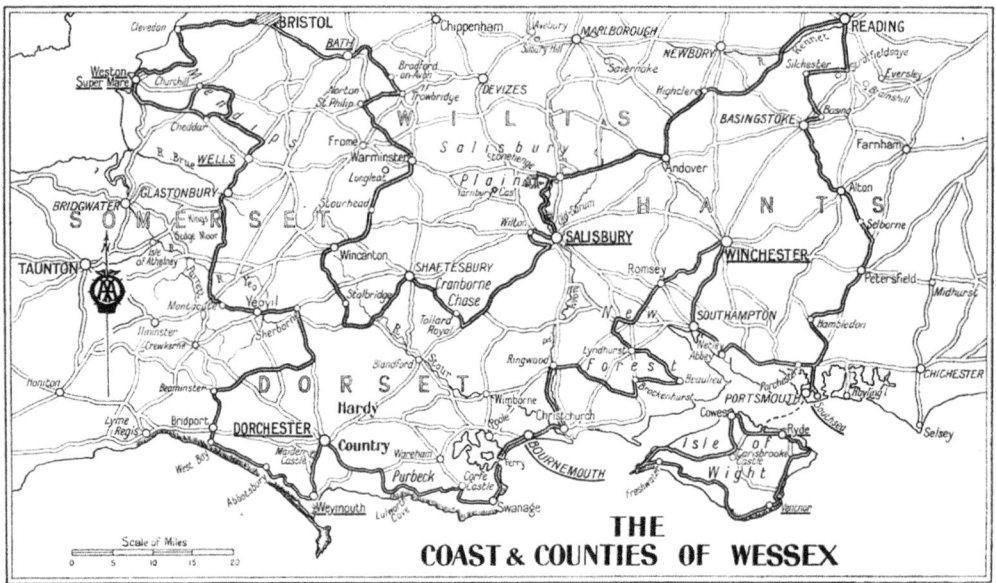

The Kingdom of Wessex

The Kingdom of Wessex

In response to the growing influence of the newcomers, between 460 and 470 a Romano-British leader called Ambrosius Aurelianus tried to impose his rather fantastic assertion that he was in control of all of Britain; as the second son of Emperor Constantine, the ruler of the Eastern half of the Roman Empire, he did have some distant claim, but other leaders who ruled various parts of Britain did not agree. Ambrosius sailed from Brittany, where he had been living after his father was murdered in Constantinople, to Devon, and led British troops loyal to him into various battles against other claimants to British rule. Various factions fought one another for years, but exactly who would claim absolute leadership was not established, even after a huge battle between Saxons and Saxon-sympathizers and Ambrosius' army was fought in 465.

This stalemate led to a long peace as both sides left one another alone, to include the Saxons ceasing their encroachment on British territory. In about 495, the peace was shattered and both sides again began to look at one another as enemies; that same year, a Saxon band, presumably looking for booty, landed on the Dorset border and this somewhat random arrival actually became symbolic of the start of a new Saxon Kingdom, *Wessex*, though the newcomers did not make any claims to land or power at that time, nor do they appear to have had any impact on Dorset.

Viking Ship

Sadly, the thirteen years of general peace between the Anglo-Saxons and the British saw a corrupt British leadership emerge, along with civil turmoil and a generation of Britons who did not appreciate the possibility of new invasions. These factors made them very vulnerable.

The Seven Kingdoms

The Angles and the Saxons agreed to divide England into "Seven Kingdoms": Northumbria, Mercia, Essex, Sussex, Kent, East Anglia and *Wessex*. Although it is not clear exactly what the boundaries of the Kingdom of Wessex were, it is known that by the 8th century its heart was in Hampshire, Wiltshire, Berkshire, Somersetshire and Dorsetshire. Each shire, which comes from the Saxon word *scir*, meaning "division of land," was governed by a "shire reeve" or *sheriff*.

This shire system actually began in Wessex, also a Saxon word from "Westseaxua rice" meaning *Kingdom of the West Saxons*; this system of land management was such an efficient way to administer local areas of a kingdom, it had been adopted throughout England, Scotland and Ireland by the 10th century.

The Saxon kingdom

Tradition has it that in 508, a Saxon king, Cerdic, arrived in Southampton where he defeated the British king NuddLludd. In truth, it is possible that there may have been other Saxon kings in this area before Cerdic's arrival, but his name remains part of the tradition of the founding, in 519, of the Kingdom of Wessex. This is supported by the fact that Saxons began arriving in significant numbers in this area about the same time, at the beginning of the 6th century. They landed on Portland, no doubt on or near the same landing used for thousands of years by earlier peoples. This group was described in the Anglo-Saxon Chronicles as "hostile," using the isle as a base to attack and pillage along the coast, but they also appear to have settled there and established small farms on Portland.

The "First" King of England

Although Wessex had many kings, both British and Saxon, there is one local king who rose to such prominence that he became known not just as the King of Wessex, but as the King of England. King Alfred the Great (849-899) is referred to in history as England's *first* king. This is because under Alfred's reign, Wessex became the largest of all the kingdoms, partly due to his enlightened leadership, but he was also the first to stand up against the growing threat to all of England's safety.

The Vikings had been conducting raids along the English coast for years, even before the fall of the Roman Empire. It was this continued and growing threat that brought King Alfred into the forefront as a national leader, as unlike other rulers who had struggled unsuccessfully against the constant attacks of those Danes, Alfred took decisive action. He chose to build new coastal fortresses and improve upon old ones, as well as assuring his army was well trained and his navy was ready to fight the Danes wherever they popped up in English waters.

Those forts included Portland's Verne (which is Brittonic for alder grove) and a smaller one located on the Eastern side of the island where Rufus castle now sits, chosen because of its strategic importance to the safety of the harbour. And according to the *Burghal Hidege*, the official document which catalogued Alfred's new defensive building, he funded the building of fortified towns all along the British coast, to include Dorset's Bridport and Wareham, with some of their ancient walls still intact today. These towns were called *burhs*, literally fortified towns, the origin of the word borough.

Alfred also understood the value of diplomacy, working with his fellow rulers in the other six kingdoms instead of fighting against them, no small feat after years of struggles and infighting between those petty kings. At home in Wessex, he was known to be a rational leader and that meant the law codes of his kingdom were based on fairness and logic; he was also a strong believer in public education and pushed his subjects to learn to read, convinced this would help strengthen his realm.

The Bowleaze Jewel

Many of Alfred's efforts helped to lay the foundation for a permanent unified England, though that journey would take another 200 years after his death.

Wessex Jewels

During Alfred's reign, he or one of his chosen representatives either lived in or visited the area around Weymouth, evidenced by the Bowleaze Jewel which was found in 1990 at Bowleaze Cove. The jewel is a gold dome that would have been attached to the top of a wood or ivory rod, almost identical to the Alfred jewel, something King Alfred is depicted carrying in all of his portraits. The beautiful ornament was made in Alfred's court jewellery workshops and is decorated with beaded wire and glass cabochon stones; it is held by the British Museum.

Saxon boys might have been called Aimon, Sigfried, Stewart, Warren, Abelard, or Odo. Popular girls names included Heloise, Archer, Bailey, Edith, Rosalind, and Yvette.

St. Augustine brings Christianity

The Christian Church had been established by the time the Romans first invaded Great Britain, but it took many years to make any permanent inroads into entrenched paganism. And though some Roman emperors did embrace Christianity, most did not, meaning as a form of worship, it was in competition with all the other religions found throughout the vast empire for hundreds of years.

By the time the Anglo-Saxons had become an established entity in England, many British were practicing Christians, having been introduced to the "new" religion by the Romans themselves. However, like the British, it also took time for the Germanic peoples to leave behind their traditional pagan religions.

The Wessex Anglo-Saxons worshipped many of the same gods as the Vikings; Thor, the god of thunder, for instance. And like the Celts, they believed in the importance of animal sacrifice. Their burial practices were also similar in some ways to those of the Durgotriges. The majority of their graves were communal rather than individual and their dead were dressed according to their status in society and the wealthy were buried with their favourite belongings, those things they needed in the afterlife.

Saxon men also believed that if they died in their sleep, they would end up in a kind of nether world, but if they died in battle, they would go to Valhalla: pagan heaven. Maybe this helps explain why the Anglo-Saxons were always fighting with one another.

The first organised attempt to Christianise the Anglo-Saxons was when Pope Gregory I sent St. Augustine, now the patron saint of Canterbury Cathedral, to England in the 590s, hoping the bishop (now saint) could shift the stubborn Saxons away from their pagan roots. Augustine's mission was to establish once and for all a permanent English Christian Church which would help turn all, not some, Britons into believers. Although his mission was quite successful, the history of Christianity in Wessex mirrors what happened during Roman rule, as Christianity waxed and waned. Sometimes the kings of Wessex were pagan, sometimes Christian. It remained personal choice rather than a matter of rule.

In fact, though there were churches scattered around the kingdom of Wessex, prior to the era of true conversion, this area could not really claim to have been truly "Christian" until the 9th century. Once that conversion happened, local believers wasted no time in building beautiful places of worship. By the 10th century these included Sherborne Abbey Church in Sherborne (though it had been a monastic centre since the 7th century), St. Martin's in Wareham, the Benedictine monastery in Cerne, and St. Nicholas of Myra in Worth Matravers. Those churches are still standing today, as are smaller churches whose Saxon foundations have been added to or built over by subsequent generations, to include St. Mary's in Radipole, St. Nicholas in Wyke Regis, Holy Trinity in Bincombe and Preston's and Portland's St. Andrews.

King Athelstan

King Athelstan (925 – 939) was the grandson of Alfred the Great and was responsible for the building of the collegiate church, which became Milton Abbey, in 933. This beautiful Dorset monastic building was dedicated to the memory of the king's brother Edmund. In order to support the church, he granted it sixteen manors around Dorset, but most interestingly, he also gave Milton Abbey 'the water within the shore at Weymouth and half the stream of that Waymouth out at sea,' with the intent of assuring the abbot and his monks had plenty of fresh fish.

Nineteenth century antiquarians interpreted the size of the gift as about half of the harbour, going all the way up to the port of Radipole, but its importance lies in the fact that this "gift" was the first time that the harbour and port were used by royals as rewards to various religious houses as well as to other royals. Having their water ways and the rights to those important resources given away was not something that was well received by the residents as it took local control out of the hands of those who made their livings from the harbour and port.

Wyke's Font

"Save us, Lord, from the fury of the Northmen!"

This was a new prayer that began to be sung in churches during Matins in the late 8th century. It was a call to God to stop the Vikings as they stepped up their attacks along the coast and inland, across England. Their determination and numbers meant that by the end of the 9th century, the "Northmen" had managed to establish their own rule over the Kingdom of East Anglia.

As the Vikings arrived in Dorset, they made life very difficult for its residents, especially those living along the coast. According to the Anglo-Saxon Chronicles, the only document that mentions these Viking raids in Dorset, two boats arrived in Portland harbour in 787; a local reeve saw them rowing toward land and assumed they were traders. To be sure that they were taken to the king to receive permission to trade in Weymouth and Portland, the reeve did his duty by having his men row him out to meet the newcomers, who promptly killed the entire party of local men.

King Alfred was far more effective in protecting his kingdom from the

Vikings than previous kings had been, though they managed to do some serious damage. In 876, his navy was patrolling the Dorset coast and came upon the Danish fleet, which was attempting to go inland via the River Brid; the British navy trapped the Vikings, preventing them from going any further up the river. The same year, the Danish army sailed around Portland and on to Poole, where they disembarked and marched on to Wareham, doing tremendous damage to that town. Alfred led his army on a chase of the marauding Danes and finally defeated them in Wiltshire.

Overall, during his reign, Alfred's proactive approach to working with the rest of the country, along with his strong navy and coastal defences, meant that Wessex was not as badly affected by the Danes as other areas of England were. Sadly, however, after his death, the kings who followed were not as successful at keeping the determined Danes at bay.

The Three Danish kings

Alfred's Navy

After Alfred's death, the reign of the new king of Wessex, Alfred's son Edward the Elder, lasted from 912 to 954. Edward tried to organise resistance to the Danes, going as far as York to overthrow the Viking king who had set himself up as ruler there. Over the coming years, each king continued an uneasy peace between the Danes and the English, but the good times ended with Aethelred the Unready (966 - 1016); the Vikings clearly saw him as someone they could push around.

In order to try to keep the peace, the new king, instead of standing up to the Danes, paid a lot of protection money. The Vikings called it *Danegeld*. The amount of money he paid indicates that Aethelred must have been very frightened in deed, as more Saxon coinage from that period has been found in Scandinavia than in England. The country was bled dry and Dorset felt the pain.

Before Aethelred had paid the Danes off, Portland was hit again by Viking raids in 982, with dozens of Danish long boats appearing in the harbour. At least 1600 warriors poured out of them and stormed up the Isle, killing and pillaging as they went. After the raid, islanders reported that the Vikings had grabbed young women as they left, dragging them into their boats. Those Portlanders never saw their homes again.

Wyck – Aethelred was the first king on record to make a gift of Wyke Regis. He rewarded a loyal minister called Atsere *Wyck* and even gave him permission to leave the land to his family at his death, rather than it reverting to the crown. It must have been an important gift given that the deed was signed not just by the king, but by the Archbishop of Canterbury.

In spite of its easy access, Weymouth and the surrounding area fared far better, with no recorded attacks there or further up the coast during this time, probably because it was much easier to defend than parts of Portland. But, Dorset continued to be affected by the Danish threat, illustrated by the fact that Aethelred was so worried about his own and his family's safety, he gave the Bishop of Winchester the monastic properties at Cerne, parts of Minterne, Winterborne, Affpuddle, Bloxworth, Poxwell, and Cheselbourne in payment for prayers to be said for them. Because of Aethelred's fear and terrible management of the country, the Vikings smelled another opportunity to invade and in 1009 they sent the army of King Sweyn Forkbeard of

Denmark to conquer England. Aethelred's answer was to flee to Europe.

King Sweyn took the throne and was followed by his son Canute, who was quick to look for treasure in Dorset. He plundered Cerne village and its church as he marched through the county. To his credit, though, he decided later to show benevolence toward the local people and returned lands held by the crown to local church rule, as well as giving back Radipole, Poxwell, Winterborne, Milton, and Kimmeridge to the local churches and landowners from whom they had been taken years before.

After Canute died, his son Harthcanute inherited the throne, but he seemed to have little interest in Dorset affairs and neither helped nor hindered the local people.

After the Danes…

What comes next is complicated, but understanding just who was related to whom is the only way to follow the continuing saga of the early kings of England and their part in local history. First, the mother of the third Danish king Harthcanute, Emma, was not a Dane, but a Norman; King Canute had "put her aside" to marry another woman and Emma, after moving back to her native Normandy, married Athelred the Unready after he fled England for exile, also in Normandy. Emma and Athelred had a son called Edward, who was later referred to as Edward the Confessor because he was supposedly a very devout and pious Christian. When Danish-English King Harthcanute died, he left no heirs and the throne returned to the Wessex Saxons when Edward the Confessor became king, his royal claim coming through his father.

> What were the Vikings called? Girls names included Aase, Bergdis, Fjorgyn, Frigga, Halldis, and Idun. Boys were called Inghram, Olyn, Hallfred, Aage, Aevar, and Eyfrod.

When Edward returned to England to claim the throne, he married Edith, the daughter of Godwin, the Earl of Wessex. Edward no doubt would have visited the local area as it contained significant royal holdings and was quite wealthy because of its harbour, sheep industry, as well as Portland's stone quarries and salt manufacture; salt was had been produced near Chesil at the bottom of Portland as well as along the marshy area of Weymouth going back to the Iron Age.

One story tells of how, after Edward accused his mother Emma of adultery only to find out he was wrong, as penance, he gave Weymouth, Wyke Regis, Melcombe Regis and Portland to St. Swithun's Priory in Winchester. These were such valuable lands that it surely "proved" how sorry Edward was to have treated his mother so badly.

A conflicting account has it that Edward actually gave Emma, not the Church, Wyke and Weymouth to show how sorry he was. This theory makes more sense, as royal records note that Edward's sister was actually the owner of Melcombe Regis and other members of his family owned Mappowder, Tyneham, and Loders, to name just a few of their Dorset holdings.

Edward's interests in this area did not end there, however; when he exiled his own father-in-law, Godwin, Earl of Wessex, for defying him, Godwin escaped to France. When he returned in hopes of overthrowing Edward, the Earl chose Portland for his return to England, arriving with a small army that attacked the island and its people. Although he made life difficult for the locals, Godwin was not successful in his attempts to overthrow the king.

Rufus Castle

HAROLD, THE QUEEN'S BROTHER

Queen Emma's brother, Harold, spent a lot of time at the King's court; when his father Godwin died, his Earldom passed to his son. Harold became Harold Godwinson, Earl of Wessex, and was now the most powerful of all the courtiers in England.

Emma and Edward did not have children, so when Edward died in 1066, he had no heir. Numerous men came forward to claim the crown was rightfully theirs, but Harold was successful in declaring himself King of England, much to the disgust of a distant French cousin of Edward's. His name was William of Normandy, better known as William the Conqueror.

The Duke raised an army in Normandy and arrived in England to challenge Harold for the throne. William based his assertion that he was the rightful heir to the throne on the fact that he was Norman Queen Emma's grandnephew *and* his claim that while in exile in Normandy, King Edward had promised to leave him the throne upon the his death.

No matter who had the strongest claim, in the end, the crown went to William when the French defeated the English at the Battle of Hastings in 1066; that same year, William was crowned king at London's Westminster Abbey on Christmas Day. He was England's first Norman king. Harold was England's last Wessex and last Saxon king.

The Conqueror's Dorset

The Bayeaux Tapestry

The Saxons introduced the concept of the royal manor, a large area of land that belonged to the monarch, worked by local tenant farmers who paid their rents "in kind," which meant a percentage of what they produced on that land: grain and meat, for instance. All those who lived on that manor land were governed not by local lords and barons, but by the king himself, through his personal agents. When William the Conqueror became king, he continued that system as well as reasserting royal claims on all royal manors to include Weymouth, Portland, Wyke Regis, and Melcombe Regis.

Viking raids did not end with Norman rule, but William was determined to prevent the Danes or anyone else from attacking his new conquest. Like those who had come before him, he appreciated the strategic location of the Weymouth and Portland harbours; he built Rufus Castle on Portland as part of his strategy of defence.

When it was built, Rufus Castle was probably quite large, possibly extending out on to a rocky outcrop that has since fallen into the sea. The castle - sometimes referred to as the Bow and Arrow Castle - gets its name from the second son of William the Conqueror, William Rufus, which means William the Red (because of his fiery red hair), who became king when his father died. This spot was important long before Norman rule, with a Saxon church and defensive fort located there hundreds of years prior to William's conquest.

The castle did not see a great deal of conflict, but during the reign of William the Conqueror's grandson, King Stephen (1135-1154) and his cousin Matilda, the daughter of William's first son King Henry I, fought over who the true heir to the throne really was. Matilda's half-brother Robert Earl of Gloucester fought her case and while he and Stephen chased one another around Dorset, Robert laid siege to Wareham, which he owned but Stephen had seized during his absence. When Robert forced Stephen to surrender, he went on to take Portland; Rufus Castle was temporarily his headquarters during his stay on the isle.

Local leadership and an expanding empire

Under William the Conqueror, the new Norman aristocracy replaced the native English elite, to include the bishops of the Church and local governing officials. This move was what determined William's long term success in controlling England and was directly related to the way he expanded and exploited the Anglo-Saxon shire system. He managed to do this in spite of the fact that even at the peak of his reign, only about one percent of the population of the country was actually Norman-born.

The new and pre-existing shires were gifted to men who had fought for him in battle or were connected to him through family ties. In return, the nobles swore an oath of loyalty to William, and were obliged to collect local taxes for him *and* to provide him with soldiers on demand.

> Norman names - Norman boys were often called William, Norman, Frank or Herbert. Common girls' names included Edna, Ada, and Ethel, which were also popular Anglo-Saxon names.

The men who received these parcels of land gained the titles of baron, earl and duke, and were known as tenants-in-chief. The common people, or peasants, of the manors were tenants of the knight, or lord, and were treated very harshly. The role of the lords was simply to keep the English people in their place, under the control of the Normans. They did not care whether the people they controlled liked them or were happy working for them and there was little the peasants could do to escape these controls; by law, they could not move away.

The effects of the Norman invasion and its ensuing feudal system were profound. Tens of thousands of men were killed in battle and hundreds of thousands of civilians lost their lives during Norman "sweeps" of the countryside. Those who could escaped north toward and into Scotland. It is estimated that before William there were almost two million Britons; after his conquest, had dropped to about 1,340,000.

The grip of Fitzgrip

In Dorset, a Norman named Hugh Fitzgrip was made sheriff in 1080 as a reward for his services to William during his fight for the crown; Hugh used his position to take the property of the local people and at his death, he owned at least 30,000 acres around the shire. He also delighted in punishing the locals by chasing them out of their own homes: when Fitzgrip came to power, there were 757 homes accounted for. Not long after his arrival, there were only 402, destroyed out of spite over the owners' dissent to Norman rule or deserted by those who ran away from it. Although the Earl of Wessex had tried early on to fight the Norman takeover of Dorset, his rebellion was crushed when the followers of both - the King and the Earl - clashed near Corfe Castle. Wessex lost.

Expensive guests- Even though the lords of the manor were quick to exploit their peasantry, the kings were also known to exploit their lords. William the Conqueror, for instance, travelled with a very large household, staying with any of his nobles that he chose to. If he decided to extend the stay it could bankrupt the lord hosting the royal party. In a few days of Christmas feasting one year William and his retinue consumed 6,000 chickens, 1,000 rabbits, 90 boar, 50 peacocks, 200 geese, 10,000 eels, thousands of eggs and loaves of bread, and hundreds of barrels of wine, beer, mead and cider.

Mrs. Fitzgrip

Hugh's wife provides an interesting look at the role of wealthy women during this era. She somehow managed to own property that was separate from her husband's, to include all or parts of Abbotsbury, Bere Regis, Buckland Ripers, Chaldon, Creech, Ringstead, Loders, Langton Herring, Martinstown, Portesham, and more.

Frutolf of Michel berg - Frutolf is called the first Medieval historian and was a contemporary of William the Conqueror. He and other European historians recorded the brutality of the Norman Conquest: *'In the same year England was miserably attacked and finally conquered by William the Norman, who himself was made king. Soon thereafter he sent almost all the bishops of the kingdom into exile and the nobles to their death; he forced the middle rank soldiers/knights into servitude and the wives of the Anglo-Saxons into marriage to the newcomers'.*

Domesday

Like his sheriff, William the Conqueror was not just brutal, he was greedy. He used his sizeable military to become the first monarch since Alfred the Great to increase the size of Great Britain, gaining parts of Wales and Scotland, as well as control over all of Ireland. He also began the formal process of surveying England so that he knew just who owned what and how much revenue he could squeeze out of his people. That national record is called the Domesday Book, a thorough census of the English kingdom and the most complete survey of its type in medieval Europe.

In it, the Domesday listed the local villages of Flete (Fleet), Chickerell, Osmington, Sutton Poyntz, Ringstead, Holwell, Shelvinghampton, Langdon Herring, Chaldon, Lewell, Mayne, Preston, Tatun (later Tatetun), Poxwell, Beincome (Bincombe), and Portland. Strangely, it does not mention Weymouth specifically, even though the first written record containing that name goes back to 934 (AD), nor does it mention Melcombe Regis or Wyke Regis. Historically, these were important centres of trade and farming, and Melcombe and Wyke were royal manors. It is probable though that this Domesday listing is a reference to Weymouth:

Amun held Wai of the Earl. Nine Thaines (men who held crown lands in exchange for their services to the King) *held it freely, in the time of King Edward, and were gelded* (a tax paid to the king) *for four hides of land* (an area of land considered enough to support a free family and their workers), *that is four carucates* (the same as a hide, approximately one-hundred acres). *In the domain there is one plough and three cottagers with one villain – have one carucate. There are two mills, which yield thirty-two shillings, twelve salt pans, and nine acres of meadow, and nine furlongs of pasture, value four pounds.*

Other Normans who land grabbed in Dorset included William the Conqueror himself, who claimed the lands that had belonged to Edward the Confessor. These included all the royal manors, Bere Regis, Whitchurch Canonicorum, Wimborne, Dorchester, Preston and Sutton. He also took the properties that had belonged to Harold when he was Earl of Dorset. Then there was the Earl of Mortain, William's half-brother, who was given forty-nine manors in Dorset, which included amongst others Upwey, Broadwey and Martinstown. Clearly, there was a lot of swapping and "sharing" going on throughout this era.

Langton Herring Village

Village names

Waimouthe means the "mouth of the river Wey" and Wey comes from the Brittonic *gwy*, meaning "slow river"; Melcombe Regis, *meoluc cumb*, is Saxon for "king's valley where milk is produced"; Wyke Regis is the "king's farm" although some have translated Wyke or *Wyck* as "a bending of the shore"; Flete is Saxon for inlet or creek; Poxwell, *Poceswylle or pochesell*, is a "rising spring of a man named Poca"; Sutton Poyntz, *Sutone*, is sometimes translated as the "farmstead of a person named Poyntz" and others translate it as "the king's land"; Preston is the "farmstead of the priests"; Osmington is the "estate of Osmund"; Ringstead, *hring stede*, is a "place near a circular feature"; Upwey, *Uppeweie*, means "higher up the River Way"; Tatetun, *Tatun*, means Tata's homestead (Tata is a Celtic first name); Broadwey, *Brodeway*, refers to the width of the river at that point; Radipole, *Retpole*, means "reedy pool"; and Portland is "an estate by a harbour." But the meaning of Chickerell? No one knows.

> What did they speak? The Normans spoke French which means that during the reigns of the Norman kings the official language of England was French. It must have made life that much more difficult for the local people as they tried to understand their overlords, many if not most of whom never bothered to learn the language of the country they were living in.

The Crusades

Only four Norman kings reigned over England, from 1066 to 1154, but during that time, incredible changes took place: the Knights Templar had begun the Crusades, a European Christian campaign which sent thousands of knights to Jerusalem and other areas of the ancient Christian world. This pilgrimage was begun as a way to keep young bored knights from hurting one another in clashes between their over lords, but popes supported it as a way to keep the holy land, in part today's Israel, free from Muslim rule. The long lasting effect of the Crusades, however, was to reopen the trade routes that had closed with the fall of the Roman Empire. This remarkable pilgrimage was joined by local Dorset men who were granted lands in order to live, prosper, and most importantly to recruit new knights to the cause.

The Knights Templar

In 1290, during Plantagenet King Edward the First's rule, the king granted the Knights Templar, by then called the Knights of St. John Jerusalem, significant lands in Dorset; they built facilities in Wareham, Toller Fratum, as well as building and farming on small holdings in Upwey, Mayne, and West Knighton, a village which takes its name from the knights who lived and worked there. They also built a church in that tiny village, which still has the emblem of the knights on its walls.

The local Knights Templar also benefited from support of other powerful men who provided money so that the knights could afford entertainment, as well as for the cost of their robes, mantles and other "necessaries," like the "brewing of beer."

Magnum Concilium

Portland's Old Church

It was possibly the Norman king's adoption of two 8th century Anglo-Saxon traditions that led to their most lasting contribution to British government. The Anglo-Saxon kings called together a Witan, which means 'meeting of the wise men,' a group made up of the kings' most important advisors and nobles. Kings did this when they needed or wanted advice about matters of government, although they were not bound to follow that advice and the Witan itself had no power to enact or change laws.

Actual power or not, the Witan's existence proves what those early kings understood: by involving leading citizens in the process of governing, they had eyes and ears around the realm. The Normans understood the value of this system and under them, it was expanded. The difference was they did not call their group of advisers the Witan; it was now the *Magnum Concilium*, the Great Council.

The other Anglo-Saxon tradition which influenced the Normans was the Moot; these were regular meetings held in each shire where cases of law were heard and important matters were discussed. Local lords and bishops of the Church, the sheriff, and representatives from each recognised village all attended and many of the decisions they made were binding. In the early Middle Ages, Melcombe Regis and Weymouth were both represented in the Dorsetshire Moot, because they were two separate villages; Portland at that time was not considered to be a town or village, therefore it did not have early Moot representation.

During Norman rule, the Moot became known as the County Court, and demonstrates the recognition, and necessity, of local representative government. These two gatherings remained separate for many centuries, but eventually the noble councillors of the Great Council and the local spokesmen of the County Court combined. The Witan, the Great Council, was the beginning of the aristocratic House of Lords and the Moot, the County Court, laid the ground work for the House of Commons. *Witan, Moot…the Houses of Parliament.*

Portland's Medieval Field System

ENTER THE "PLANTA GENISTA"

The death of King Stephen (1135-1154) brought an end to Norman rule. The new king, Henry II (1154-1189), was the first of the next English dynastic line: the Plantagenets. The name, however, may have been new - it was simply the nickname of Henry's father, who always wore a sprig of broom, *planta genista,* in his cap - but Henry's mother Matilda was the granddaughter of William the Conqueror.

In 1150, at the death of his father, Henry became ruler of Normandy and Anjou. In 1152, he married Eleanor of Aquitaine, the wealthiest heiress in Western Europe. The next year, traditional history tells us, he crossed to England to pursue his claim to the English throne. It seems more likely however that Henry was simply sailing along the Normandy coast with a small force of his men when a winter gale hit them, driving them across the

59

Channel and onto a Dorset beach. This theory is supported by the fact that Henry's force was very small, indicating he was not intending to invade *and* no one who understood the difficulties of travelling across the Channel during the winter would have tried such a silly thing.

Henry II was known as a king who did his best to make his mistakes work - he was good at bluffing, in other words - and finding himself on either the Sandbanks or Weymouth beach, he made it seem as if this were a planned visit. It worked and the following year, he reached an agreement with the childless King Stephen to succeed him at his death, which occurred in 1154.

When he became king, Henry II inherited a country that was in the middle of a civil war; English lords had built castles without the kings' permission and were gaining more and more control over their local territories, fighting one another for land and the people who worked it. It was very much like the era right after the fall of the Roman Empire, when there was little or no central control, demonstrating just how unsuccessful the last Norman kings had been. Henry II, yet another French king, re-established central rule over all of England and Scotland, while maintaining control over Normandy and Anjou. By 1169, he began a long and bitter battle to control Ireland, which had slipped away from the Norman kings. It did not regain self-rule until the twentieth century.

Henry's iron clad rule over so much territory helped to rebuild the waning powers of Great Britain and it was during his reign that the jury became an important part of British law, but as time went by, all was not well within his family, especially with his powerful mother.

Eleanor was the Duchess of Aquitaine, a wealthy kingdom independent of France until Eleanor married the King of France, Louis VII, when her land became his. She was a truly unique woman and not just because of her wealth and position; she accompanied her husband when he was asked by the Pope to go on the second Crusade, the second pilgrimage of the Knights Templar. Unlike the first Crusade, this one was a total failure when Muslim forces defeated the Knights in Turkey. During this trip, Louis and Eleanor fought constantly; the couple had had two daughters together, but no son, which Louis blamed on her. He made it clear to Eleanor, who had by then inherited her father's kingdom, that he wanted to pass his crown on to a son, not a daughter.

Louis and Eleanor were divorced in 1152 and only two months later she married Henri of Anjou, who became Henry II of England two years later. He was 19 and she was 30.

French wine…

When Eleanor married Henry, her lands left French hands and became English territory, firmly establishing the English king's rule in another kingdom bordering France. The vast wine industry of Aquitaine was now able to export large quantities of wine and brandy to England, which meant the ports of London, Southampton, Poole and Weymouth saw the ancient - and lucrative - importation of wine, which had begun during Roman rule, re-established. The Close Rolls of numerous Plantagenet kings list huge shipments of French wine to Weymouth. They also describe the fines levied on local ships' captains who tried to avoid paying taxes on that wine.

The Life of Stone

Because of its abundance, stone was at the heart of local life for millennia, but the early records refer to quarrying and shipping Portland's limestone to other areas; its local use and the people who built with it are rarely mentioned. Obviously, though, going back to at least the Romans, men were working with local stone and are the forebears of later craftsmen who came to be known as "stone masons."

Saxon masons left their mark as the builders of the first Christian churches of Dorset, but little is known of the lives of medieval stone masons. As the centuries ticked by, however, more and more stone structures were built – abbeys, castles, town walls – and that meant the need for lots of stone masons and the development of this trade as a recognised profession. But traditional histories state that masons were not "local" workers, they were men who travelled from place to place, following the work as it became available, the most famous example of this being the magnificent cathedrals. Cathedral records help to document the fact that masons did have to follow the work – a number of records for various cathedrals list the names of the head masons, which included the surname Dorset – but there were certainly highly skilled builders working with stone who were unlikely to have followed the bigger projects. There was no need.

The 12th and 13th centuries were busy times for the local masons, as they built beautiful little churches in many of the local villages. In the 1170s, masons constructed both Wyke Regis' All Saints and Osmington's St. Osmond's; other villages whose stone churches were built in that century include Bincombe, Fleet, Radipole, Maiden Newton, Bere Regis, Upwey, Warmwell, West Knighton, and Broadmayne. Many of these were built over existing Saxon churches.

The building continued into the 13th century with Owermoigne, Little Bredy, Wakeham, and Upwey, followed in the early 14th century by Preston and Broadwey, where again, the Medieval church was built over earlier Saxon places of worship. And though local history refers to most of the limestone used to build all of these churches as "Portland stone," some of it actually came from the small quarries of Upwey, Portesham and Preston.

Easton Village

Eleanor and Henry had five sons, proving her first husband wrong for blaming her for not having a male heir, and three daughters. For nearly two decades, besides having eight children, Eleanor played an active part in running Henry's empire, both of them travelling back and forth between their territories in England and France. But Henry and Eleanor's sons mistrusted each other, made worse by their father's policy of dividing land among them instead of leaving it all to the eldest. This practice is called patrimony and led to Eleanor's involvement in two of her sons' plotting against their father.

When Henry found out, he imprisoned his wife to stop her from meddling in the family fight over who should succeed him. When Henry died in 1189, their son Richard became King Richard I, better known as Richard the Lion Heart because of his bravery in battle. He freed his mother and when the new king went off to fight in the third Crusade, she, not the arguing brothers, ruled England in Richard's place. Only ten years later, in 1199, Richard died in battle and was succeeded by his brother John.

Wakeham's Old Church

John's Dorset

The reign of King John (1199-1216) was also not a peaceful one, and like his father Henry II, John loved Dorset and spent as much time as he could at his local properties. He had hunting lodges in places around the county, to include Cranborne Chase, Tollard Royal, Bere Regis, and Dorchester, where he kept his hunting birds and many of his finest horses. Like the kings before him, John found ruling England difficult; his powerful lords vied for power, some of them even wanted to replace him. When life at court became too much, he gathered up his royal entourage, along with all the royal jewels and monies, and headed for Dorset; he felt especially secure at Corfe Castle where he could get away from a restless Westminster. The castle was a much safer place for a king with enemies and he could spend his days hunting. John rode his prized horses along the Purbeck coast, all the way to Weymouth.

King John's troubled rule saw one of the most important events in

English history take place: he was forced by his barons to accept the Magna Carta, a document which subjected the king to the law of the land for the first time in history. Although there were no signatories from Dorset who witnessed the original document, when it was confirmed during Edward First's rule (1297), Dorset was very well represented. The Abbots of Cerne, Sherborne, Abbotsbury, and Milton all signed that version of the Magna Carta.

Southwell Village

Portland balks...

During the Middle Ages, farmers allowed their lands to go fallow by rotating their crops and leaving one section at a time unplanted, which required breaking fields up into three sections. Portlanders, however, favoured a two-field system. The lack of trees meant they had to use dung as fuel and the resulting shortage of manure to feed the land made it necessary to leave half rather than a third fallow. Each field was divided into a large number of strips, usually an acre or half an acre each, then separated by unploughed banks which were called balks; some of those are still visible near Southwell. The resourceful Portlanders did not waste an opportunity, though, they grazed their farm animals on the unused fields.

Nine Widows…

The account rolls of the "manor of Portland" tell a great deal about life on the Isle. Those records, for instance, demonstrate laws and customs relating to marriage, inheritance, criminal behaviours, and widowhood. Between 1248 and 1249, Robert Waleys paid the lord of the manor fifteen denarius to give his daughter Sabina in marriage within the manor. In other words, if a man wanted to marry his daughter off to a fellow Portlander, the father had to pay a fee, similar to a dowry. Reginal White paid two shillings for a heriot, an inheritance fee, which allowed him to take over his father's holding when he died. And Robert Rede had to pay a bit more for the same.

A widow could also keep her husband's holdings by paying a heriot; nine Portland widows paid two shillings each to secure their homes and land. The manorial court also collected fines for a number of offences. Thurmond paid six denarius for pouring short measures of ale; Adam Chep paid the same after being caught "brawling," as did Gilbert Waleis for building a wall without permission.

> Thirteenth century Money – A 13th century pound was equal to £532 pounds in the 21st century, the shilling was equal to £27, and the denarius - always represented as "d" - was equal to about £2.22 in today's money. For some reason, it was only the denarius whose reference was never Anglicised, it simply became known as the penny, now pence. Other coins remained true to the originals: schilling is derived from the Latin "solidus," a disk used as coinage; and pound, which comes from "pondo" meaning weight, is still used today.

The manor accounts also document monies paid for kitchen and dairy equipment, as well as wages paid for four ploughmen, a Hayward, a shepherd, and a dairy woman. One pig and one ox along with wheat were donated to the harvest boon day, a traditional celebration held after a series of days or weeks during which the peasants of the manor had worked for free for the lord to bring in his crops. On this occasion, there were 360 "men at harvest" to feed. Those accounts also document that the manor sent via horse cart to the lord Prior of St. Swithin's Priory in Winchester a porpoise, two loads of conger eels and another load of fish, worth a total of 24 shillings. It is a wonder that fish would be fresh after such a long journey.

> Stranger- The Durotriges refered to the strip of land connecting Portland to the mainland as the Kamber, from Brittonic *Camb*, meaning crooked or curved. This is probably where the unique Portland word for stranger, Kimberlin, comes from.

The First Charter

The reason the manor of Portland was sending produce to faraway St. Swithin's priory was because of the long association the local area had with that religious house. Weymouth harbour was granted to St. Swithin's by Edward the Confessor in 1046. In 1110, Henry I granted both the 'ports of

Weimuth and Melecum' to St. Swithin's indicating that either the king was so happy with the priory's management of the harbour he decided to award both sides to the monks or he was unaware that the monks already owned Weymouth's port. Almost two hundred years later, in 1240, the priory was granted the right to hold a market and fair in Weymouth by Henry III.

Then in 1252, the prior awarded Weymouth's inhabitants their first charter, granting the harbour the status of a 'free port.' The borough was also granted "free" status and entitled to immunities and privileges few communities enjoyed at the time. That same year, 1252, the prior of "St. Swythuu's," William of Taunton, visited "Waymuo" with his secretary, who recorded just what parts of the community looked like at the time. In his description, looking toward Portland from Rodwell, there were a few houses near the Ferry, with a long, high shingle beach, and back toward Weymouth, he described a rough track running through 'Melcombe common,' toward "Darchester Way."

A new cathedral – Exeter cathedral was rebuilt beginning in 1265; by 1300, Portland stone was imported to help complete the huge Gothic structure. The cost of the stone? Ten shillings, or about £260 in today's money.

A few years later, the priory sold the estate of Weymouth, Portland and Wyke to the bishop of Winchester, who in turn in 1259, exchanged them for lands in Oxfordshire owned by Gilbert de Clare, the Earl of Gloucester. De Clare's estate was passed on to his son, who already owned a part of Wyke Regis. It was his heir who built the first wind mill in the area, around 1304, which probably stood on or near the harbour, not far from Smallmouth Bay.

Soon after that first windmill, others began to appear and milling became an important profession throughout Dorset, to include the Weymouth area. A windmill in Wyke Regis was recorded in 1314, also the property of Gilbert de Clare. Melcombe Regis's windmill was near the town common and Portland had many, some from the same era, with more built around the Isle up to the late 18th century, to include two in Weston and at least one in Southwell.

Local millers were part time workers, often balancing their milling with fishing, net making, and other trades. The wheat, rye and other grains they ground were locally grown and the loaves they made were often huge, feeding entire families; bread was the primary staple in most local people's diets.

Portland Windmill

St. Ann's Church, Radipole

THE LULL AND THE LONG WAR

Edward III (1327-1377) was yet another English king who had claims to the French throne; when he tried to enforce those claims his efforts added to the political conflict which led to what became Europe's longest conflict. The Hundred Years War, the modern term for a series of conflicts which took place over 116 years, was fought between England and France. The origins of those fights went back to the Norman (French) conquest of England.

When King Louis X of France died, Edward claimed his throne based on the fact that the king left no direct heir and that Edward's mother Isabelle was the daughter of the French King Philip IV and sister to the now-dead King Louis. Edward's was a reasonable claim, given he was the closest living male relative to Louis, but the French nobles had different ideas and were not excited about having "another" English King. They crowned a cousin of

Edward's instead and then attacked Edward's lands in Aquitaine. This is when the English king decided to declare war on France. It was 1337.

To fight and win the war, Edward decided he needed a strong navy; he is often called the Father of the English Navy. He asked all coastal towns in England to give him ships and Weymouth was not only one of the few willing to donate to its king, the town gave him 20 ships and 264 sailors, more than any other in the country. They may have been so willing to help because that same year, the French attacked the Dorset coast and left many seaside towns in ruins.

In 1338, Edward declared himself King of France; in response, the French again sent ships to the Hampshire and Dorset coasts, sacking towns like Portsmouth, where everything was destroyed except the hospital and a church. Returning in 1339, Portland was hit hard, but Weymouth and the surrounding villages were not attacked.

When Edward and his army returned from France in 1344, his ships landed in Weymouth. Although it is not certain, it is possible that he actually sailed on one of the ships that had been donated to him by Weymouth. It is also possible that, ten years later, the horrible scourge that temporarily stopped the long war was also carried on one those ships. The people of the 14th century called that scourge the *Great Pestilence*.

'In this year, 1348, in Melcombe in the county of Dorset, a little before the feast of St John the Baptist, two ships, one of them from Bristol, came alongside. One of the sailors had brought with him from Gascony the seeds of the terrible pestilence, and through him the men of that town of Melcombe were the first in England to be infected.' Grey Friar's Chronicle, Lynn

Edward III fought a huge battle in Gascony, one of the two provinces in France owned by England; as the Chronicle states, one of the ships that landed in Weymouth's harbour in 1348 was carrying a sailor from that region and he may even have been a veteran of that battle. Either way, when the *Great Mortality*, the *Terrible Pestilence*, arrived in Britain by way of Melcombe

Regis, the contagion was already spreading across all of Europe. This terrible calamity was also known as the *Great Plague* and the *Black Death;* today we call it the *Bubonic* - from the Latin word *bubo* which means 'swelling of the groin' - *Plague*, a horrible disease carried by the fleas of black rats, which travelled in the holds of merchant ships. The fleas bit humans, infecting them with the disease.

As soon as it arrived, the contagion spread like wild fire across Dorset, which was quickly dubbed the *Plagueshire,* as it was not just the first to be affected, but the hardest hit in England. A contemporary described the county: '…many villages and hamlets were desolated, without a house being left in them, all those who dwelt in them being dead.'

According to the Salisbury Cathedral Records, Dorset lost at least half its population, but the single group hardest hit was the clergy. In just seven months after the onset of the plague, one hundred Dorset priests had died. The first victim was a vicar living in Chickerell, followed quickly by two priests from St. Mary's (now St. Ann's) Church at Radipole, then the vicar of Holy Trinity in Bincombe.

The seventh year after it began, it came to England and first began in the towns and ports joining on the seacoasts, in Dorsetshire, where, as in other counties, it made the country quite void of inhabitants so that there were almost none left alive. From there it passed into Devonshire and Somersetshire, even unto Bristol, and raged in such sort that the Gloucestershire men would not suffer the Bristol men to have access to them by any means. But at length it came to Gloucester, yea even to Oxford and to London, and finally it spread over all England and so wasted the people that scarce the tenth person of any sort was left alive. Geoffrey the Baker

Void of inhabitants

Before the plague hit, Weymouth and its surrounding villages had vibrant wool, wine, and milling trades, but because the lands had passed from the Church to the monarchy during the grandfather of Edward III's rule, most of the area's residents were suffering under the strain of the high rents demanded by the king. Wyke Regis, Radipole, Melcombe Regis, Portland, and the rest of Dorset all saw their rents go up and up.

Because so many people died during the plague, there were not enough workers to take care of the farms, the farm animals, or to make milk and cheese, to fish, or to perform other vital tasks. The work force was so diminished by the disease, Edward ordered his local sheriff to prevent any Portlander from leaving the Isle. This was an attempt to keep the survivors working the quarries, the land and the sheep farms; it was also a way to assure no food supplies were taken off of Portland, to be sold to people in Weymouth at inflated prices.

Just as worrying, this lack of able bodied adults meant that all along the Dorset coast, the sea defences had no one working them and Dorset was considered to be at risk from another invasion from the French. That fear was realised when French and Spanish ships returned again to Portland in 1404 and 1405. The English navy simply did not have the resources to patrol and keep the entire Dorset coastline safe. Given the fact that even by the 16th century there were only about 400 people living on Portland, it is not difficult to see why its people were such an easy target.

Chronicon Angliae

Although the plague was the worst disaster that had ever happened to England as far as loss of life, it did, strangely, have some positive long term effects. With the loss of half of the population, there was a desperate lack of workers, both skilled and unskilled. Survivors of the epidemic discovered that they could demand higher wages, and in some cases made enough money to get out of the semi-slavery that many peasants had to endure after the Norman Conquest, even buying land of their own or moving away to seek a new life. This was the first major social and economic shift in hundreds of years. But that does not mean that Dorset recovered quickly. It took years for the population to grow and to thrive. It was still struggling into the 15th century, when both Weymouth and Melcombe Regis had to ask King Edward IV for tax relief.

> **Dorset's cloth making industry**: Although Weymouth, Melcombe and Poole were better known as the ports from which unrefined wool was exported to Europe, there were busy mills producing woollen fabric in and around Dorset going back to at least the 11th century. The Domesday Book notes two of them in Weymouth. By the 1600s, the local area was still producing not just wool, but there were fields of flax which fed linen mills, farms dedicated to growing hemp for the milling of heavy cloth to make boat sails, and there were even silk mills.

Dorset Smugglers

Although going back to the Anglo-Saxon kings who demanded payment in kind - mostly military service - from their subjects, it was not until 1275 that taxes on goods produced in England were formally introduced. Weymouth and Melcombe Regis had their own customs collectors, appointed by the king in 1303, to make sure all that export wool was accounted for and brought in plenty of revenue for the crown. Because of its importance to the kings of the 14th century, Weymouth was made an official wool export port in 1314 and remained a vital source of royal income, along with the many royal farms like Wyke Regis, for generations to come. Its importance only grew as kings added to the list of taxable goods; wine, which had not been taxed for generations, followed wool.

From these new taxes arose a new "profession": smuggling. And nowhere in the kingdom was there a better place to be a smuggler than the Dorset coast.

Early Tax Avoidance

Initially, the tax was quite low, but by the reign of Edward III, with his greater and greater demands for money to fund his wars in France, the costs of importing and exporting grew. As taxes and Dorset residents' love of imported wine and brandy also continued to grow, and local wool's popularity remained strong in Europe, any opportunity to buy and sell without paying taxes was welcomed.

Not to be confused with pirates, smugglers were individuals who found ways to sell goods without the king's representatives' knowledge. That is why smuggling got its start in the 13th century: medieval tax avoidance. Throughout Edward's reign, more and more local smugglers got into the act; sometimes they paddled out in tiny boats to ships moored along the coast, using burning rushes or candle light to signal the ships' captains to let them know they were coming. The goods were loaded and the smugglers disappeared back in to the night. The craggy Dorset coast was perfect for this activity, especially along the western edge of Portland, with its rocky and dangerous coastline.

The fact that there were far too few custom's officers to patrol the rough ground and there were lots of quarries to provide hiding places for both men and goods made it a smuggler's paradise. Elsewhere, all along the coast, there were tracks leading inland which meant a fairly wide variety of villages where the illegal wines, brandies, and even food stuffs could be stored and sold on later. Some publicans were quite open about their smuggled drink. For instance, only a few years after the permanent custom's duty was placed on wine, locals knew that if they wanted French brandy, the pub in Osmington Mills was the place to buy it. But smugglers were not the only people who took advantage of the wild Dorset coast to help themselves to ships' cargoes.

La Michel

Even before custom's duties, in the 12th century the abbot of Abbotsbury was given permission by King John to send the monastery's monks out to the beaches whenever there had been a ship wreck; anything that came off the ship belonged to the abbot. This led to plenty of people, including churchmen, not only gathering up the spoils from ship wrecks, but causing them, hence the term *wrecking*.

The Dorset coast is so hilly, one or two men could stand on the edge of a rise waving a burning rush; ships' captains, especially if they were having trouble in a storm or in heavy winds, would see the light and head for it, hoping to find safe harbour. Instead, smugglers were waiting to board the vessels and to take everything they could carry. This often led to grisly murders of seamen and passengers who resisted, and if the ships were not considered salvageable or were made so in order for the *wreckers* to cover their tracks, they were burned. At least one such group of bad guys was caught.

In 1362, Edward III's son, Prince Edward of Wales and Aquitaine, sailed from London, planning to stop in Weymouth to re-provision his ship, *la Michel*, which was loaded with the prince's household goods and on its way to either Wales or France. The captain, a local man called Richard de Preston, ran into heavy weather off the Dorset coast.

Unlikely to have known whose ship it was, a group of local *wreckers* "many men of Waymouth, Melcombe and other parts entered the ship, carried away said goods…and burned the ship." When King Edward found out about the incident, he ordered the Dorset sheriff, Thomas de Bridport and another local official, Nicholas de Poyns, "to make inquisition" and to return the stolen goods to Captain de Preston, who obviously survived the attack. The Prince's goods were to be safely stored until the "king give further order, certifying him in the chancery of the nature and value of these."

There is no record of how the captain and the prince got off the ship safely or what happened to the wreckers, but obviously they were caught and the stolen goods returned to the rightful owners. Few other ships' captains were so lucky.

Soldiers and Mariners

As the local towns and villages recovered from the plague, the harbours continued to be vital to the export of locally produced wool and the import of European wine and other goods. But when it came to the local ports, Edward III valued them just as much for their *other* purposes. Radipole, Melcombe Regis, and Weymouth were centres for recruitment and transport, providing men the king needed to continue his struggle for control of much of France.

The year 1377 was a very dramatic one for Dorset. In early May, Edward sent his *Admiral of the "Southward Fleet"* Welshman Guy de Briene, to Weymouth. The king had given de Briene large tracts of Dorset land in return for his services, which included many trips to the ports of Weymouth, Melcombe Regis and Radipole where he was ordered to find "men-at-arms, armed men, archers and mariners" to fight in the ongoing Hundred Years War.

The admiral's search for military was not really "recruitment" in the modern sense, however. The king's agent sent his own men-at-arms into the community to identify any male physically able to fight; if he resisted, those soldiers were commanded to "arrest all who are contrariant, seize their lands and goods into the king's hand, and commit their bodies to prison until the king give further order touching their punishment." This practice is eventually called impressment.

Radipole Village

Between 1350 and 1377, the records show that the village of Radipole alone sent 184 archers to fight in France; others came from Osmington, Upton and the Weymouth area. Considering how small the population was at that time, more so because of the long term effects of the plague, this was a huge portion of the male population.

The Merchant Knight

In spite of the hardship the recruitment of so many men must have caused for the local people, wool remained a crucial part of the Dorset economy and continued to be the number one export to Europe from the Weymouth and Melcombe Regis ports. The king's admiral was one of the biggest producers and exporters of wool in the county. In recognition of his successes providing so many men-at-arms, Edward agreed to let De Briene, sometimes spelled DeBrian, take control of the Dorset lands that were inherited by "underage" boys - by law, when an estate went to a male child, the king could claim that land – adding to what he had already been given and making the Welshman both very powerful and very wealthy, a wealth based on taking men away from their families to fight in a war they knew little or nothing about.

The Archer

Those who served and fought for their king, the knights of the realm, did not associate themselves with the buying and selling of goods; they considered it beneath them. But Admiral de Briene broke that mould and the royal records show him referring to himself as a 'merchant.' After that, the reference caught on and created a new rank in English society: the gentleman merchant. It caught on to such a degree that even the sheriff of Dorset during the 1370s became involved in the wool trade and also referred to himself as a merchant. After all, if the king's man could do it, why not other "aristocrats"?

Did children have jobs? Yes, they did, and some of them were really awful. For instance, because wool was such an important export grown locally and shipped out of the ports of Weymouth and Melcombe, there were quite a few fullers working in Dorset. A fuller is someone who treats the wool so that it is soft and shiny. And the children's job? Fuller's apprentices were little boys who spent their days treading around on top of piles of wool in large vats full of human urine, which contained ammonia and gave the wool a nice soft texture.

Who were the Johns?

Two of de Briene's Radipole recruits were archers John Smyth and John Large, both of whom managed to survive numerous campaigns in France, over at least two decades, returning after each to resume their work in their home village. There is no record as to just what they did for a living, but they did pay their taxes, which provided the evidence of their survival. These men clearly had last names that preceded the 14th century, which is when surnames became a necessity so that the crown's tax collectors knew who had paid their taxes. Large comes from Old French for "generous," Smyth from an ancestor who worked as a smith and their first names were taken from the Bible: St. John. The name John was the most common boy's name during the 14th century. If they had been archers in previous centuries, they would have been John Archer and John Archer; or, if they had not come from a family with an identifiable profession, they might both have ended up being John de Weymouth or John de Radipole, as surnames were also derived from where the man or his father or grandfather had been born and lived.

May and June...

The last time Edward III ordered his admiral to recruit in Dorset to fight his war was in May, 1377. The following month, on the 29th of June, fifty French and Spanish ships, loaded with 4,000 soldiers and a quantity of guns and cannons, crossed the English Channel and sacked the West coast of England. Weymouth was one of the worst hit; upon arrival, the admiral who commanded this enemy siege, a Frenchman named Jean de Vienne, ordered that everything that could be burned should be. Other towns badly damaged included Portsmouth, Plymouth, and Dartmouth; it was not until the French and Spanish troops marched ten miles inland toward Lewes that this invasion was stopped and the foreign forces were pushed back toward the coast. A few days after this terrible event, the king, who was suffering from dementia among other ailments, died, leaving a country suffering from the ongoing threat of French invasion and excessive taxation.

The King's liege

The kings who followed Edward were not as interested in Dorset as those who had come before, mostly because between the plague and the destruction of Weymouth, it was not making the kind of money for the monarchs it once had, and the French and Spanish remained a threat for years to come. But it was not money that brought the local communities to the attention of the king, this time Henry IV (1366 – 1413), it was what happened after the next French attack.

In 1404, a French fleet invaded Portland. Oddly, the only reference to this new invasion 15th century chroniclers bothered to record was that the French had landed but "were repulsed." That was not, however, the whole story. The French were not chased away, they were captured by the king's lieges, men who were required to serve their local lord and their king. These local representatives of the king were accompanied by his clerk, a man named Henry Shelford, who just happened to be visiting Weymouth on the king's business and was informed of the French arrival. There is no record as to what the French were carrying on their ships, but it turned out that it was the Frenchmen themselves who were the valuable cargo; the sailors, soldiers and their officers were taken prisoner and held for ransom.

When the French crown paid the ransom in return for those prisoners, however, there was a problem. There were more lieges than there were prisoners, so not everyone got a share of the reward; apparently they had each grabbed a prisoner of their own and those who were not lucky enough to have one did not get any money. The men who missed out made such a fuss, complaining loudly to the local sheriffs about how unfair it was, the officers took the complaints to the king. Henry responded personally: "Thomas Cole of Weymouth and John Penne of Portland to levy from the captors a tenth part of the ransom of the prisoners taken in the victory by the king's lieges over certain of the king's Norman enemies who lately entered the realm near the Isle of Portland, and to distribute the same among the rest of the king's lieges who took part in the conflict but did not take prisoners there…"

Hides and wood fells

Although there were continued reports of French "pyrotes" harassing individual homes and farms along the Dorset coast, especially along the Purbeck, life in the 15th century was reasonably quiet compared to the 14th. When King Henry V ascended the throne in 1413, he took up the French cause again by attempting to take back lands lost to his predecessor. Weymouth and Melcombe continued to be amongst the busiest ports both for the exportation of wool and the importation of European goods "both of wools, hides and wool-fells and of the 3d. in the pound and other petty customs in the port of Melcombe."

And under Henry V, these were again busy exit points for the military. From about 1413 to the 1420s, he regularly ordered his sergeants-at-arms to take ships "and mariners for the passage of the ambassadors of the king's adversary of France now within the realm and the king's ambassadors and their servants, households, goods and harness to France in the ports of… Melcombe and Weymouth." The most commonly mentioned French ports of call for the ships leaving from Dorset were Brittany, Aquitaine and Gascony, not surprising given the crown's long relationship with those states.

The Cult of St. James

Henry V also gave permission for another kind of travel from Dorset. Beginning in the early 1400s, pilgrims were leaving from Poole harbour to celebrate the Feast of St. James, who was supposed to have been one of Jesus' disciples. This patron saint of labourers visited Santiago, Spain, where he died. Pilgrimages were encouraged by the Church during the Middle Ages, the most famous in history being those made by the Knights Templar during the Crusades. The pilgrims from Dorset were not knights, however, just devout Christians who believed that by making a pilgrimage to an important shrine they would either be forgiven for all of their sins or that the shrine's saint would heal their diseases or other afflictions. Although there were plenty of churches in England that claimed to hold the bones of various saints, going to all the trouble to make a pilgrimage to another country showed that the penitents were truly devoted to God.

The popularity of making pilgrimages continued to grow throughout the 15th century. They were a mixture of Christian devotion and wanderlust. In 1428 alone, there were eleven of them, with 926 pilgrims, 122 of those from Weymouth. In 1413, 1429, 1434 and 1445, "Leonard of Weymouth, a balinger" (a small single-sailed boat used for coastal trade, designed to carry forty people) carried passengers Nicolas and James of Weymouth, someone with the odd name "Holy Ghost of Weymouth," along with dozens of other locals who all took part in various pilgrimages, most departing from Poole.

There was at least one pilgrimage that did not leave from Poole, however, and was apparently such a big deal, those wishing to make the journey had to ask for the king's permission. King Henry VI gave "Licence for

Pilgrim's boat

John Gower of Weymouth to conduct sixty pilgrims in his barge, called la Lenard de Weymouth (the same balinger that left from Poole) to, Samtiago of Galicia." Given that there were statues and busts of St. James at both Sherborne and Milton Abbeys, it is likely that there was a local cult dedicated to his worship and those sixty pilgrims found it more convenient to leave from Weymouth than from Poole. There is no record of who they were or if they ever made it home, but it must have been quite a trip.

Sandsfoot Castle 1790

THEN COME THE TUDORS....

Understanding the life and times of British kings and queens can be confusing at best, and the 15th century is no exception, but it was a vital time in the history of Dorset, especially given what happened in 1422 when Henry V died and his infant son became Henry VI. Unlike his father, this Henry was never a strong king, he was more a pawn stuck between two wealthy families, both vying for control over the crown. Those families, the Houses of York and Lancaster, both felt their leaders should be king and that squabble became known as the War of the Roses. Henry IV, V, and now VI were all from the House of Lancaster and the Yorkists were determined to end that line of succession.

After Henry V died, his widow, Catherine of Valois, married a handsome Welshman and one of Henry V's squires, Owen Tudor. Tudor was a staunch supporter of his stepson Henry VI and in 1461 led an army into battle against Yorkist forces at Mortimer's Cross in Herefordshire. The Yorkist side won, Owen Tudor was killed, Henry VI lost his throne and the Yorkist claimant, Edward IV, became king. The House of Lancaster was never in power again.

> **St. Laurence's** – The 13th century church of St. Laurence's in Upwey played host to Henry VI's queen, Margaret of Anjou, when she landed in Weymouth and was taken to the church to rest before going on to Cerne Abbas. When her husband was killed, she returned to France.

Before he was killed, though, Owen Tudor had several children with Catherine of Valois; one of those was Edmund Tudor. He married Margaret Beaufort, who was related to John of Guant, the third son of King Edward III. Edmund and Margaret had children of their own, and the eldest was Henry Tudor. When the last of the Yorkist kings, Richard III, was killed in battle in 1485, Henry seized his chance and through his claims to Edward III, became Henry VII, the first Tudor king. Henry's rise to power spelled the end of the War of the Roses, helped by the fact that he, a descendent of the House of Lancaster through his mother, married Elizabeth of York.

Henry VII and Dorset

Henry VII obviously realised the importance of defending the Weymouth and Melcombe harbour and built a defending castle near what is today the Nothe. But it was a Dorset man's influence that brings this king into the local story. The first Tudor king's reign was a very successful one, thanks in part to the fact that he listened to the advice of his Lord Chancellor, John Morton. Morton, who was made the Archbishop of Canterbury in 1486 and chancellor the following year, was born in the tiny Dorset village of Milborne

St. Andrew in 1420; he pursued a career as a church lawyer, and made his way through the ranks to become an intimate of the king. He realised that Henry's claims to the throne through his mother, Lady Margaret Beaufort from Kingston Lacy in Dorset, were not very strong; he was, in the minds of many, a king by conquest, not heredity. It was Morton who convinced Henry to strengthen his claims by marrying Elizabeth.

Compelled by tempest

During the reign of Henry VII, Weymouth had two important royal visitors: Philip I, the king of Castile, and his queen, Joanna. The royal couple had been in the Netherlands and were on their way to Spain where Philip was about to become king, when the three ships carrying them and their possessions were separated from the other seventy-seven ships in the huge royal and military flotilla; they were blown off course during a terrible storm in the Channel and eventually landed in Weymouth, or as a local chronicler put it they were "compelled by tempest to put into port of Weymouth" on 10 January 1506.

When locals saw the foreign ships coming, they quickly prepared to defend the town, sending a representative to the local governor Sir Thomas Trenchard, to inform him of the pending attack. Not realising what a panic they had caused, the king and queen demanded their ships land so that they could rest and get over the horrors of being thrown about in such a bad storm. They assumed they could come and go without any one of importance realising who they were. The governor, however, had acted quickly and sent news to London. Henry VII immediately dispatched 300 soldiers to the governor's residence outside of Dorchester and the Spanish royals were escorted to meet Trenchard there.

Scarʃte of healpe- The 1432 rolls of Parliament document two petitions sent to the king from the leaders of Melcombe Regis. They were asking the eleven-year-old Henry VI for help, a plea that demonstrates the never ending problem the local communities suffered from 'enemies':

"To our soverayne Lord the King plese it to your Royall highness . . . [that] your porte of Melcombe [suffering from] . . . scarste of healpe of pepole to . . . resyst the . . . ennemies . . . [whereas] your towene and havon of poole is well . . . manned and there ys a sewar . . . Poole Harbour haven . . . wheare yo' mayor and burgesses ben fully purposed, yo' gracyos lycens Harbour there to had, to walle incarnell <a wall with battlements> and fortefey yo' sayde towne . . . [wherefore the petitioners pray the King] to annull the sayde porte of Melcombe . . .The coinons ben assented to this byll . . ." which was to take effect "at the feast of saint illerey net coming."

It was signed Joheʃl Olever. Although much of the spelling is idiomatic, it appears that the local leaders were hoping that the king would fund the building of a new wall that would help keep enemies out of Weymouth and Melcombe Regis.

Meanwhile, the governor was very concerned over the fact that neither he nor any member of his staff spoke Spanish and the Spaniards spoke no English. He remembered, though, that his nephew who lived outside of Bridport had travelled extensively in Spain and spoke fluent Spanish. That nephew, John Russell, was assigned to translate for the king, and Philip I liked him so much, he asked to have Russell accompany him to London. Here they met the English king and Russell became a member of the royal household. After Henry VII died, Russell stayed on and served Henry VIII, and then, King Edward VI, who made him the Earl of Bedford, where the Dorset man made his own great fortune. So, an accidental trip that could have ended in disaster actually ended with a treaty signed between two powerful kings agreeing to a trade partnership and another local man becoming one of England's most powerful leaders.

***

When he died, Henry VII left a strong, stable country with a growing economy, but that was not enough for his son, the new king Henry VIII. This Henry wanted even more for, but mostly from, his country, his subjects. To include those who lived in Dorset.

Life in Tudor England

Like the eras before, the economy of Tudor Britain (1485 to 1603) was based mainly on agriculture with the majority of the population living and working the land, but it was also a time when English society was experiencing tremendous change. The population was expanding and towns began to grow quite large; especially in the late 16th century, trade and industry expanded making aristocrats and the middling classes richer and richer. Towns like Weymouth and Melcombe, because of their ports, were part of this growth. But like most eras in history, there were winners and losers in Tudor times.

As the standard of living improved for the wealthy, their homes became quite comfortable. There are two Tudor houses still standing in Weymouth and those demonstrate how substantial middle class homes had become; they were made from Portland stone and contained fireplaces, quite a new concept at the time. Prior to this period, most homes had wooden frameworks and for those who could afford it, open hearths that vented straight up through the roof, not ideal as they may have vented the smoke of a fire, but the heat was also escaping through the big whole, while snow and wind could come down it.

Mrs. Johnson's House near Weymouth Harbour

For the labourers, however, life simply became harder. That was partly because of the increase in population: at the beginning of the 15th century, the English population was about two and half million; by 1525, it was up to over three million; and by 1600, it had passed four million. That rapid rise meant as those centuries ticked by, there were often more workers than there was work and the labourer was no longer a highly valued commodity, unlike the post-plague years.

"I receves allemes"

English law had changed in the previous century, making it legal for the working classes to move away from their places of birth; this was quite a common practice by the Tudor era, but not necessarily because people hoped to find a better or more interesting life. People were most likely to move away from their home towns, villages and farms to look for work, not to explore the world around them.

If those job seekers could not find work, some became vagrants, moving from place to place, begging instead of working. The best place to beg, of course, was in a city, town or large village, where there were established churches, town governments, meaning plenty of people to beg from. The residents of the growing towns, who were seeing a huge increase in transients, were not happy about one of the results of this movement: they did not like having poor strangers hanging around and considered their presence a danger to the town's people as well as the town's reputation.

Henry VIII's parliament passed some drastic laws to try to limit this human movement and made begging illegal without permission of the local government. Anyone who wanted to beg had to request a special licence to do so. Then there were laws that required local governments to provide for certain classifications of the unemployed; locally, the "crippled," widows, and others who could not do traditional types of work were provided with locally grown wool, flax or hemp, for instance, in order for them to make something that they could sell.

Vagrancy was apparently a very big problem in Dorset, especially locally. Even into the 17th century, the Melcombe borough archives of 1617 to 1631 listed cases of vagrants "whipped and sent away by a passe" and the local marshal was paid very well "for the great pains and care" he had given "in searching out and apprehending rogues and vagrants at fairs and other great places of meeting within this country."

Then came the Tudor workhouses, built to house both vagrants and locals who became homeless; they were forced to stay in these places and to work at whatever tasks they were considered capable of doing. These were very bleak places, and the conditions within the workhouses were awful. To add to the humiliation of being so poor, in some areas, to include towns in Dorset, anyone who was reliant on help from the local town government was required to wear a badge made from either metal or heavy course fabric with the words "I receves allemes" written across them, to be sure the townspeople knew just who was homeless and without work.

Schooling in Tudor England - Because it was big enough to support one, Weymouth had a "petty school," where a teacher, sometimes a woman, instructed children whose parents could afford the tuition, in very basic skills, to include reading, writing, etiquette, and the catechism. The sons of the upper middle classes were taught at home or at Catholic monasteries; they learned to read and write in English and Latin, along with studying maths and religion. Wealthy girls, however, were rarely taught anything beyond sewing, music and sometimes religion; poor girls were not taught anything that was not useful to their families, which meant learning from their mothers how to cook, sew and run a household. During the Tutor era, only about ten percent of men could read and write and only one percent of women could do either, proof of how rare an education really was.

If a vagrant refused to work and live in the workhouse, the local sheriff or his representative was empowered to beat him and to brand his right ear, another way to be sure everyone knew his or her shame. If caught trying to beg in the same area again, the sheriff had the right to hang the vagrant. The law that allowed for this level of capital punishment of poor vagrants was repealed in the late 17th century as too harsh even for the times, but the use of the badges lasted until the 1700s.

Did Henry VIII ever sleep here?

Although he is often thought of only as the king who married – and divorced – many wives, Henry VIII did a lot more than that, much of which had a profound impact on Dorset.

Portland's Castle

Henry's first queen was Catherine of Aragon, but because their only child was a girl, and Henry wanted a son to carry on his reign, he tried to divorce her so that he could marry someone else. This angered the Pope who would not grant the divorce; instead of listening to the head of the Church, though, Henry decided not to recognise the Pope's authority and divorced his wife anyway. This meant that England was no longer connected to the central Christian Church, leaving it isolated from the rest of Europe. Right after Henry's divorce, France and Spain signed a trade and defence treaty, which left Henry, like kings before him, worried that his country was at risk from the union of these traditional enemies. In response to his fears, in 1539, he funded the building of thirty defences around the English coast, to include Portland and Weymouth. This was the biggest coastal defensive programme since the time of the Anglo-Saxons.

Henry ordered a survey done of the Dorset coast in 1539, and based on the information it provided, he decided that one fort would not have been sufficient because the cannons of the time had very limited range. Henry was a student of history and he no doubt knew that both places had been attacked in the past not only by the French, but by Vikings and even earlier invaders.

The forts were built on the harbour, Sandsfoot Castle in Wyke Regis, Portland Castle on the edge of Portland's harbour and Cotton Fort in Melcombe Regis (a much earlier defence that was improved for greater protection). Sandsfoot and Portland were known as device forts, meaning they were designed so that cannons could be placed facing into the harbour, allowing the two castles to work together to stop any enemy boats before they could land their soldiers along the beaches or the causeway.

In 1544, Henry's concern over the growing threat of the French, led him to do what his predecessors had done before; he demanded Weymouth provide him with men and arms:

Henr. R.

Trustie and well beloved, we greate you well. And whereas betweene us and the

Emperor upon provocation of manyfolde injuries committed by the Frenche Kyng unto us both particularlie; And for his confederation wyth the Turke, against ye whole commonwealth of Christendome. It ys agreed that eche of us aparte, in person, with his puissant Armie in several parties this soommer, shall invade the Realme of Fraunce; and being not yet furneyshed as to our honour appertayneth:

We have appointed you to send us the nombre of xv hable fotement, well furneyshed for the warres as appertayneth, whereof iii to bee archers, every oone furneyshed with a goode bowe in a cace, with xxiii goode arrows in a cace, a goode sworde, and a dagger, and the rest to be billmen, havyng besides theyre bill, a goode sworde, and a dagger, to be levyed of your owne servants and tenants.

And that you put the saide nombre in such a redyness, furnished with coats and hosen of such colours as is appointed for the battle of our Armey.
As they faile not within oone houres warnyng to march forward to such place as shall be appointed accordinglie.

Yeven under our Sygnete at our plaace of Westmr., the fifth daie: of June, the xxxv of our reigne. Henr. R.

Given neither the French nor the Spanish tried to conquer England during his reign, perhaps Henry was disappointed he had spent so much money on the castles, but the impact of having to again provide men and supplies to the king would have had quite an impact on the community.

Portland's Old Battery

Ducheman…

Henry VIII spent a lot of money during his reign and that meant higher taxes for his subjects. The tax records from this time document who paid what, but they also tell the story of just how many people who were not English-born lived in the Dorset area. That is because the king decided that a good way to raise more funds was to identify "aliens" and charge them twice as much tax as native Englishmen. It turns out the Weymouth area was quite culturally diverse.

In 1525, for instance, there were about forty "aliens" living in Weymouth, Melcombe Regis, Sutton Poyntz, Owermoigne, Wyke Regis and Portland. Some were Normans, others included "Ducheman, Frenscheman," but the majority were not identified as far as origin, they are simply identifiable because they paid double taxes. The primary trades the aliens worked in were in the production and exporting of wool, as well as weaving.

There were also carters, men who hauled building materials to large construction sites, which makes sense given all the building being done in Dorset during Tudor times. Others were mariners, and especially in Weymouth living and working along the River Wey, there were dairymen. These were Norman and Dutch; they had arrived with a long history of fine cheese and butter making from their own countries and found the local grasses perfect for excellent milk production. The location was also ideal because they could export their goods from Weymouth's port to other parts of England and even to Europe. Interestingly, all the aliens identified by Henry's tax men paid the high taxes, while a large percentage of Dorset natives were too poor to pay any tax at all.

> **Inkell** - Dutch weavers introduced the "Dutch loom" to the English weaving industry in 1610; it worked with a "wheale, wherewith one man could weave twelve times as much" making Inkell, or inkle, a narrow strip of fabric such as ribbon or belting. It was in common use by local weavers in Weymouth and surrounding villages as early as 1624.

Henry's antiquarian

Henry VIII was a very educated man and he understood the importance of reading; he considered it a necessity to maintain a large royal library and he employed a very interesting royal librarian to manage it. That person, known as the Keeper of Royal Libraries, was called John LeLand, who beside his position as Henry's chief librarian, was also an avid historian, then called an antiquarian.

This librarian was a very curious man and wanted to know just what was happening in and around his own country. His interest combined with his passion for the past led Leland to travel from shire to shire to learn more about each area's past and present. Beginning in 1535, he went on an eight-year-long fact-finding journey, talking to locals and writing about their towns and villages. In doing this, he created a record that otherwise would not exist. His work included detailed notes on some of Dorset's towns and villages.

Leland, for instance, wrote about the River Wey; his description is further documentation of the fact that what is now just a marsh was once a very busy river, ending near the village of Radipole, which in turn had once been an important inland port. He also documented that some local people called the river the Wile, not the Wey.

Henry's Map

The Antiquarian's Milton

There are many Saxon and Medieval villages that have been "lost," some now just farm land, others with a church or manor house still marking what was once a bustling community: Dewlish, Steeple, Fleet, Warmwell, Frome Billet, Lewell, Mayne, Upton, Little Bredy, Bhompston, Bincombe and Ringstead, to name just a few in the immediate area. But it is surprising how many of our lost villages were literally swallowed up by their neighbours, rather than actually being deserted.

Tatetun and Holwell are now part of Chickerell, which is itself now a part of Weymouth, and Broadwey, Preston, Upwey, Wyke Regis, Sutton Poyntz, and Melcombe Regis were also consumed by Weymouth. Chesilton on Portland is now part of Fortuneswell, and also on Portland, Rayfourth (sometimes Ralphton) would have been near Weston. Then there is Bridge, a tiny settlement on the Chesil Bank, across from Wyke.

Leland demonstrates how problematic it can be to interpret just what chroniclers of the past were trying to document. He refers to Milton as a village, but he is actually talking about Melcombe Regis: *Ther is a townlet on the hither side of the haven of Waymouth caullid Miltoun a being privileged and having a mair. This toun, as it is evidently scene, hathe beene far bigger then it is now. The cause of this is layid onto the French-men that yn tymes of warre rasid this towne for lak of defence. For so many houses as be yn the town they be welle and strongly buildid of stone. Ther is a chapelle of ease in Milton. The paroch chirch is a mile of: a manifest token that Milton is no very old town.*

Tudor Weymouth and Portland

Leland also records how the residents of Weymouth and Melcombe went from one village to the other: "and the trajectus is by a bote and a rope bent over the haven; so that yn the fery boote they use no ores."

The Dominicans

There are many beautiful churches in Dorset, some with roots going back to the Anglo-Saxons. This area certainly had and still has its fair share of those important buildings which reflect both local and national history. But there were also some very important religious communities in Dorset: Sherborne, Milton Abbas, Abbotsbury, Bindon, Cerne Abbas, Wool, Forde and Christchurch are some of the best known. However, there was a very important friary in the local area, one that was also documented by John Leland.

"Ther was a fair house of Freres in the est of the twon: and the chief house of the Rogers in Dorsetshir was founder and patrone of it. "

There were three distinct groups of friars serving the Church and all three, the Dominicans, the Franciscans, and the Cistercians, were represented in Dorset. However, local history has not always celebrated the very last Dominican friary to be established in England; it was built in Melcombe Regis in the 1430s.

All three orders believed that it was important to build religious communities located in places where the members could serve their community by working directly with the towns or villages residents. These religious communities were called "open houses," meaning their members lived as part of the greater community. When a local knight, Hugh Deverell, decided that Melcombe and its inhabitants were not faring very well during the early 15th century, he decided to contact the chief of the House of Rogers, John Rogers, whose Dominican order lived in Bryanston, just above Blandford Forum.

When these men who wanted to help the local community applied to build a friary with its own church along with a belfry and cloister dedicated to St. Dominic in Melcombe, they were given permission by the head of their order. After beginning the project, the Bishop of Serum, whose bishopric was responsible for the local churches, decided to rescind that agreement. This meant that Rogers and Deverell had to go over his head and speak directly to the Bishop of Durham, who secured them royal licence to finish the project.

The Dominicans' decision to build their friary in Melcombe was based on the belief that the town was in "dissolution," meaning it had lost its centre, and because there was no place "dedicated to God": the closest parish church was in Radipole, built in the 12th century and now Weymouth's oldest building, but a mile and a half away. Although Wyke Regis had had a chapel since the 10th century, which had been rebuilt in about 1260, and there was a "chapel of rest" in Weymouth, these were tiny buildings and did not offer the full complement of church services.

The religious men felt that by building a holy community in the centre of town, the friars could help locals who they considered "rude, illiterate, and situated in angulo terrae (end of the earth)." Not a very complimentary image.

Wyke Regis and its Church

Rogers and Deverell were also concerned about outside threats from the French or other invaders, a fear fuelled by the fact that during the 15th century, the "vill lay open to enemies, whereby the king's rent was not paid and the customs were diminished." In other words, this coast was open to attack and that ongoing problem had taken its toll on the people and the economy. The fear of French invasion, as well as pirate attacks, meant that the friars did not just help feed, clothe and educate the people of Melcombe Regis, they also built a jetty and assisted in constructing a "defence of the town," which included a manned tower used as a lookout to protect residents from marauders.

In order to achieve all of this, the friars asked King Henry VI to grant them another area of land running along the sea front - free from any rent - and a monthly stipend which came from the customs' duties taken at Poole harbour.

The riches of the House of Rogers friary - The friary's belongings were inventoried just before the order was disbanded and indicates it was not a wealthy. The items listed included "a fair table follt of beyond sea work," new stalls, new altars, seven images, six marble stones, new seats at the Jesus altar, and a bell in the steeple. The inventory does not include anything remotely comfortable, like beds or arm chairs, but the friars did have a few trinkets to include small gold rings, some silver jewellery, a silver chalice, and a Holy Rood.

Wyke's new church

Wyke Regis has had a place of worship in the same location at the top of the village since at least the 10th century. In about 1260, that was replaced by a more modern stone building. All Saints, the village's current church, replaced that one in about 1455 and was made of Portland stone. It contains some of 13th century church's stone carvings. Examples of that early work which can still be seen today include a gargoyle-like figure who is suffering from toothache, a face playing a pipe whistle and depictions of other early musical instruments. There is also a dog with his bone, a carving that actually predates the 1260 church, and a builder holding his hod, a V-shaped open trough on a pole, used for carrying bricks and other building materials. The church yard was once much larger than it is today, but apparently it was still not big enough for all the bodies the parishioners wanted buried there. That is evidenced by the fact that the vestry was once an occuarium, a room where bones were stored when old graves were dug up to make room for new bodies.

Wyke's church was clearly an important part of the village for centuries and after the completion of the 15th century structure, it remained Weymouth's central church into the 19th century, evidenced by the memorial carvings dedicated to some of the local coast's most dramatic ship wrecks up through to the late 1800s.

Henry's dissolution

Henry's problems with the Pope had a devastating effect on the religious houses of England and Wales. Not only had he broken away from the Vatican-led Catholic Church, paving the way for the creation of the Church of England, during Henry's time as king, the European Catholic leadership was actually fighting over who the rightful pope was. This struggle became so complicated that at one point there were three men simultaneously claiming they were the real pontiff. This and the fact that there were many people in England and Europe who were calling for the reform of what some saw as a deeply corrupt Church, meant troubled times for Christianity. But what were the reformers unhappy about?

Indulgences

Many of the big monasteries in England and Europe had, over hundreds of years, become very wealthy. They owned huge pieces of land, most given to them by wealthy patrons, and they often made money from wool and other goods produced on their lands; their leaders sometimes had the right to force local peasants to labour for them for free, meaning even more money in the pockets of the monasteries. Also, most bishops were willing to accept men and women who had no interest in serving the poor or doing good deeds but simply had wealthy parents who paid the Church to take their children into religious orders.

Those parents saw serving the Church as a respectable profession for a second or third son who would not inherit the land or for a daughter who was unlikely to marry well. But the most controversial thing the Church "indulged" in was *indulgences*; this was the process of selling prayers and promises of salvation. Imagine if someone from the local community wanted to assure that she would go to heaven, she could go to the priests or monks and they would accept money in exchange for prayers assuring her safe passage. Although many people were convinced this was a good use of their money, there were others who recognised it as a very corrupt, impossible, business deal.

Abbotsbury's Church

Henry VIII knew how wealthy the big monasteries were and his right hand man, Thomas Cromwell, who wanted to control the monastic lands to increase his own power and wealth, capitalised on both Henry's greed and his hatred of the pope; Cromwell lied to the king, telling him that much of the money made by the monasteries was being sent directly to the Vatican. He knew this would be a great excuse for Henry to use to close the religious houses down. In 1536, an act was passed by parliament allowing Henry to do just that.

By 1540, only four years after he had begun his move to eliminate the religious communities, over 800 monasteries had been closed. In Dorset, that meant the abbeys at Sherborne, Shaftesbury, Forde, Bindon, Milton Abbas, Abbotsbury and Cerne Abbas were sold off, redistributing their land amongst those who had helped Henry to close them and to those he owed favours. For example, in 1541 Sir Giles Strangways, the Earl of Illchester and one of Henry VIII's commissioners for the dissolution in Dorset, was given the 11th century Benedictine Monastery at Abbotsbury, together with its extensive lands, the Fleet running all the way into Wyke and the swannery. The estate has remained in the Strangways family ever since.

Another beneficiary, John Tregonwell, a lawyer who had assisted Henry VIII in obtaining a divorce from Catherine of Aragon, bribed Cromwell and was allowed to purchase Milton Abbey and some of its estate; he paid £1,000 plus a rent of £12 per year for it. A few months after buying the abbey, he gave the church to the town's people as their parish church and took up residence in part of the old monastic buildings. Despite the fact that the country had become Protestant, he and his family still practiced Roman Catholicism, which stood him in very good stead when Queen Mary ascended the throne. He was knighted during Mary's coronation and made Sheriff of Somerset and Dorset.

Favourite Tudor names - The most popular boys' names were John, Thomas, Henry, Edward, Richard and William. Favourite girls' names included Anne, Elizabeth, Catherine, and Mary.

Sherborne Abbey's story was similar; it was closed on 4 January, 1540, and given to Sir John Horsey, one of Henry's knights. Horsey sold the abbey two months later to the local people to be used as their parish church; it remains so today.

Abbotsbury's Convent House

The sad news is that shortly after being closed, abbeys like Abbotsbury's fell to ruin very quickly. After the monks left, local people broke up the buildings in order to reuse the stone. That is why so many of the formerly grand buildings became mere shells soon after the dissolution. Those churches given over to local people for worship rather than sold off to profiteers were the lucky ones, and continue to be important places of worship for their local communities. The Dominican friary's church buildings in Melcombe did manage to survive, but by the end of the 16th century, they were in very poor condition and eventually torn down. The monks themselves were pensioned off, leaving no trace of the good works they had done for the community.

> **Recycling churches** – Sandsfoot Castle was built in part out of pieces of stone from the dissolved Bindon Abbey near Wool. When restoration work has been done on the castle, various carvings dating from the 12th century have been uncovered throughout the building, all recycled from the once-great Medieval abbey buildings. Lulworth Castle was built over the abbey of Bindon.

Elizabeth I

In spite of his fights with the pope, when Henry died in 1547 he left only one son, Edward VI, who was a sickly child and only lived to his early teens. After a great deal of infighting between the politicians of the time over which of Henry's daughters held the true claim to the throne, Henry's eldest daughter Mary became Queen Mary I. Mary was born in 1516 and became queen in 1553; she married the King of Spain, Phillip II in 1554, and died a few years later, in 1558. Enter Queen Elizabeth I, Henry's youngest daughter.

The First Protestant Tudor

Elizabeth's reign was full of intrigue, violence, religious tension, but especially, she was the first English monarch to see the possibility of great riches both on the high seas and in the New World. It was during her reign that the British began in earnest their historic journey in becoming the world's most powerful empire.

Elizabeth I (1533 - 1603) inherited a government that had been torn apart by political struggles and a deeply divided church; she was the first Protestant British monarch, but she was careful not to erase all traces of Catholicism and retained, for example, the traditions of candlesticks, crucifixes and clerical robes in English Protestant churches. By pursuing a policy of religious moderation, she attempted to maintain the status quo. This annoyed the Puritans, a severe new sect within Protestantism, who were particularly upset by the continuance of some Catholic traditions, but

Elizabeth was able to create an uneasy compromise between all the religious factions, something she worked hard to maintain throughout her reign.

> **Sup not loud of thy pottage** - The Elizabethans had a very strict set of rules when it came to table manners, some of which are familiar today: *Dip not thy meat in the saltcellar, but take it with a knife. *Belch near no man's face with a corrupt fumosity <wine breath>. *Eat small morsels of meat; eat softly, and drink mannerly.
>
> *Corrupt not thy lips with eating, as a pig doth. *Scratch not thy head with thy fingers, nor spit you over the table. *If your teeth be putrefied, it is not right to touch meat that others eat.
>
> *Wipe thy mouth when thou shalt drink ale or wine on thy napkin only, not on the table cloth. * Blow not your nose in the napkin where ye wipe your hand. *Chew with your mouth closed.

'I am already bound unto a husband which is the Kingdom of England.'

Although it was not customary for a woman to rule, Elizabeth did so with passion and commitment to her realm; she also determined never to marry, possibly because as the daughter of Anne Boleyn, Henry's second wife, she had lived through the horrors of her parents' painful marriage and of her mother's beheading. She also expressed a dread of being told by a man how to do her job as queen, though Elizabeth was never short of suitors wanting to marry her, all hoping to become king; even her former brother-in-law, King Philip II, proposed to her, though it had nothing to do with love. He simply wanted control over Britain.

Civic Pride

Between 1568 and 1569, Melcombe Regis' leaders borrowed enough money to build an impressive town hall. Weymouth already had a hall built earlier in the century, but it followed suit by revamping that structure in the early part of the 17th century. These were notable buildings for their time, with the upper floors containing council chambers where officials met on town business and guilds could also hold their meetings. There were rooms for storing arms, plate, minute books, charters and other corporate possessions. Weymouth's hall contained the town gaol on the underground level and Melcombe's probably housed a small school on the upper floors.

Weymouth's Old Town Hall

It was quite rare for towns and villages as opposed to cities to have such impressive public structures, but Dorset was a leader in that kind of building in the 16th and 17th centuries, with Milton Abbas, Cerne Abbas, Poole and many other small communities building their own civic facilities. Besides being symbolic of quite a prosperous era, the timing of this building is significant: the importance of the village church as the centre of civic activity was being replaced by publicly owned halls. Even the fact that Melcombe's new building had a cupola which later held a clock is symbolic of the replacement of church bells as a way for the town's people to know what time it was.

A View Across Chesil Village

THE TOWNS THAT COULD NOT GET ALONG....

'Commission to Guy de Brian, Ralph Spigurnel, the king's admiral, Westminster, and William Tauk to make inquisition in the county of Dorset Touching the complaint of the king's burgesses of Melcombe that, whereas a society of the water of Weye, running between their town on the north and Weymouth on the south, from the thread in the middle of the water, and the soil beneath it, pertain to the king and his crown from the thread thereof as far as the said town, and ships, crayers and boats have come to the said town and put in there freely and without impediment time out of mind, and paid dock-dues (cullagium) and customs on their goods, until they were of late hindered by the men of Weymouth, tenants of Lionel, duke of Clarence, the king's son, the said tenants now claim all the said water and all the soil beneath it, and also all the port of the said water between the two towns, permit no ships, crayers or boats to put in within the lordship of Melcombe, and attract to themselves all the profit which would pertain to the king if the said ships put in to his said lordship.' The Calendar of State Papers, Edward III

Elizabeth's reign had a tremendous impact on the local communities when in 1571 she, through an act of union in Parliament, combined

Weymouth and Melcombe Regis into a single town: Weymouth. This decision was based on the hundreds of years of their bickering over access to the harbour. Going back to Edward III, the people of the two communities had been taking their troubles all the way to Parliament, something Edward had tried to take care of by sending his admiral, Guy de Brian, to settle the on-going disputes. Even that powerful man had not succeeded.

The townspeople's arguments arose mainly out of complicated claims over who owned the rights of way to the River Wey's channel; both wanted control over that access to benefit their own merchants and ship owners, but they also wanted the power to charge arriving ships for access. The struggle for control over access became so acute, it caused, according to a 16th century antiquarian, "much trouble to the Queen and those have governed before her and a great decay and impoverishment to the town." In 1571, Elizabeth and Parliament made the decision to combine the towns into one, believing that would solve the problems. Many locals were very unhappy about the change, especially those living in Melcombe. And, one town or two, the residents continued to argue between themselves until they were physically joined by a permanent bridge over the channel in 1594, which apparently helped calm the situation.

Religious dissenters - Between 1587 and 1594, six persons were put to death in Dorchester because of their religious opinions. The severe penal statutes of the time meant that after they were executed, their bodies were quartered and put up on poles for public viewing in Upway, Sutton, Preston, Osmington, Wyke, Winfrith, Broadmayne, Radipole, Piddletown, Bincombe, Winterbourne, and Weymouth.

In 1598, Elizabeth again focused on Weymouth when, through an act of Parliament, she appointed the mayor as the crown's local representative and justice of the peace, but even more significantly, she gave Weymouth the right to elect four members of parliament. This meant that, with the exception of London, it was the only single borough at the time to have such a right, a nod to the importance of the harbour and its strategic location for both national and local defence and the economy.

The Anglo-Spanish War

Elizabeth and Phillip of Spain were former in-laws, but they were also fierce rivals. As English privateers like Francis Drake and Walter Raleigh rose in prominence at court because of their successes at sea, many of which involved capturing rich Spanish cargoes for their queen, the Spanish king became determined to end the growing strength of the English. Besides his concerns over those privateers, the Spanish king was also unhappy about English explorations into the New World; he did not like the direct competition over the growing trade possibilities with all the rich raw materials being discovered there. Adding more fuel to the fire, Phillip was also anxious to put an end to Elizabeth's desire to help spread Protestantism in Europe, specifically her assistance to the Dutch who were trying to break away from the Catholic Habsburg Empire, which was controlled by the Spanish. In 1579, Phillip decided to invade Flanders to stop the Dutch break away, which Elizabeth continued to support; his plan included attacking England.

In response to the growing Spanish threat, an English fleet was pulled together and of those fifty ships, six were supplied by Weymouth. They included the Galleon, captained by local man Roger Miller; the Golden Lion, captained by Thomas Howard; the Sutton, captained by local man Hugh Preston; along with the Expedition, the Catherine, the Ark Royal and the Heath Hen. These were charged with both patrolling the Dorset coastline and defending against the Armada at sea.

Although the Armada proved to be an awkward collection of poorly piloted ships that stood little chance against the smaller, lighter English fleet, when it was sighted entering the Channel, people living along the Dorset coast must have been terrified. They saw the warning beacons along the southern coast being lit to warn residents of a pending invasion, and would have had no idea that their own navy was in full pursuit. They had been warned that Spain was a threat and many were concerned that if they chose to, the Spanish could land at Portland Roads, where they would be out of reach of the guns of Sandsfoot and Portland castles. Because of that concern, two years prior, the local beacons had been inspected, a gun platform had been erected on Portland overlooking Chesil Beach, and some local men were equipped

The Spanish Armada at Portland

with weapons and powder. One hundred soldiers were also stationed there to provide extra protection.

When the two country's fleets met, the first of the Spanish ships to fall to the English was the San Salvador, which was the paymaster's ship, not a war vessel. English cannons had started a fire on board, which in turn caused the ship's ammunitions to explode, killing many of the sailors and soldiers on board. The San Salvador was hauled into Weymouth harbour, but not before locals managed to take most of its cargo. What was left was supposed to be removed by Carew Raleigh, Sir Walter Raleigh's brother, and given to the community to help build up their defensive stores. The locals never received those weapons, however, and they somehow mysteriously ended up being sent to London instead. The ship itself was intended for refitting, but when being moved to Poole, it sank off of Studland, which was probably because the new sail ordered for it had not been fitted.

Coastal Beacon Blazing

The remaining Armada clashed at Portland Bill with the English fleet on the 23rd of July 1579; winds made it difficult to engage and the battle was not decisive, though the English ships, lighter and captained by far more experienced leaders, harried the Spanish who found the treacherous rocks, high winds and competing currents at the Bill too much in their large, cumbersome ships. The English managed to avoid those problems because they had captains from the local area who knew how to navigate the obstacles.

The salvagers did not get all the paymaster's coins. Over the centuries, lucky local children continued to find Spanish coins, called "ducky stones," washed up along the shores of Chesil Beach.

When the battle ended, there was no clear winner, but the Armada was much worse for it, eventually making its way back to Spain with only half of its original ships and one-third of its men, most of whom were diseased and starving. Beyond battling the English fleet, those men sailing with the Armada had been getting by with very limited rations and were already in a weakened state before the engagement.

Although many local people had watched the amazing battle from Portland's cliff edges, there were also some who actually got involved, loading up their small fishing boats with any kind of ordinance available, all hoping to help the English sailors win, though just how they would have reached the ships as they manoeuvred around and shot at one another, sending massive cannon balls back and forth, was not recorded.

Elizabeth's Water

Sherborne Castle's Gardens

Sir Walter Raleigh may have been one of Queen Elizabeth's favourite privateers - she called him her "Water" - and he was involved in a variety of battles against the Spanish during the Anglo-Spanish War, he did not take part in the Battle of Portland. This was because at this point Elizabeth did not trust his judgement in dealing with the Spanish, although his ship, the Ark Royal, which Raleigh had designed himself, was the lead ship in the battle.

The queen may not always have trusted Raleigh, but in 1592,

Elizabeth made him the Captain of Portland Castle, which he declared was ill equipped to deal with the continued threat of Spanish invasion to Dorset shores. He also became a local Member of Parliament in 1597; his interest in representing the local communities would not only have been because he owned Dorset's Sherborne Castle, but also because he and those who worked for him sailed in and out of Weymouth harbour on a regular basis. Many of those trips involved Raleigh's exploits in the New World.

Ruins of the First Sherborne Castle

To find those people which were left there in the yeere 1587 ...

Although Elizabeth and Raleigh's relationship was often a stormy one, some even believed he had hoped to marry her, the queen was very fond of her Water and when he asked her for something, she rarely said no. That was true when he applied in the 1570s for permission to explore and claim land in the New World. She granted him that right, but his first attempt in 1582 barely made it out of Plymouth harbour before having to return. He tried again in 1584, when he sent a group of men and women whose job it was to create a permanent settlement that would help to establish English presence in the New World and hopefully, make Raleigh a very wealthy man. That settlement is now called the Lost Colony of Roanoke.

Once again in 1585, a ship sailed for the New World, but this time it left from Weymouth; it carried over 100 employees of Raleigh's who were under orders to set up a working colony. This attempt at temporary colonisation failed when supplies ran out and relationships with the local native people went sour, but it was Francis Drake, also exploring the shores of the New World, who found out that Raleigh's colony was in trouble and he rescued the surviving colonists, returning them to Portsmouth. Raleigh did not know about Drake's kindness and it was only when he sent his own supply ship to the colony that he found out it had been deserted. Raleigh tried again, but was not successful.

> **MP Raleigh** - As usual for Sir Walter, all was not smooth sailing after moving to Dorset; he was a man of letters and loved to have lively philosophical discussions with his learned friends. This led to the religious leaders at Cerne Abbas, long the local home of Church leadership, to suspect him of being an atheist. This was because of his outspoken religious beliefs which did not always mesh with the traditional Church of England's doctrines. Ever the orator, Raleigh managed to talk his way out of the charges.

On one of his early trips, Raleigh had enlisted the well-respected Elizabethan mathematician and scientist Thomas Hariot to explore just what kind of resources the East coast of North America had to offer. Hariot's discoveries turned out to be vital to Raleigh's effort because though like others before and after him, Raleigh's first hope was to find the same kind of gold reserves Spanish explorers had discovered in South and Central America, when that precious metal was not found, the scientist did find plenty of native plants that were considered to have excellent medicinal qualities. These were highly valued by English and European apothecaries.

The Capital – Raleigh was so confident his efforts would result in permanent English settlements in the New World, he noted that he wanted the capital of the first colony he was trying to establish to be named Raleigh. Oddly, his name is the only evidence of his many attempts to colonise: the capital city of the American state of North Carolina is called Raleigh.

Enter Mariner Mace

Samuel Mace of Weymouth, a very sufficient Mariner, an honest sober man, who had beene in Virginia twise befoe, was imployed thither by Sir Walter Ralegh, to finde those people which were left there in the yeere 1587. To those succour he hath sent five severall times at his owne charges. Their owne profit elsewhere; others returning with frivolous allegations. At this last time, to avoid all excuse, he bought a barke, and hired all the company for wages by the moneth: who departing from Weymouth in March last 1602, fell fortie leagues to the Wouthwestward of Hatarask, in thirtie-foure degrees or thereabout; and having there spent a moneth; when that the extremitie of weather and loose of some principall ground-tackle [anchor and mooring tackle], forced and feared them from searching the port of Hatarask, to which they were sent.

From*:* "A briefe Note of the sending another barke this present yeere 1602, by the honorable knight, Sir Walter Ralegh, for the searching out of his Colonie in Virginia" by John Brereton

Hariot's work is significant to local history because it reveals Raleigh's actual purpose in returning to North America, and it also brings to light a long-lost local character. His name was Samuel Mace.

Mace was a master mariner from Weymouth who went on, and led, at least three of Raleigh's exploratory trips to the New World which sailed from Weymouth harbour. His story helps to document the great privateer's "true" intent in sending parties of settlers to the New World and relief ships to Roanoke.

With each of his expeditions, Raleigh continued to claim he was only trying to find the people of the Lost Colony of 1587; that had not changed by the time his men took what turned out to be the last trip sponsored by him. In 1602 Raleigh supplied the expedition with another barke, a two or three-masted merchant's ship, which was commanded by Mace "who had been at Virginia twice before, and was employed by Sire Walter Raleigh to find those people which were left there in this yeere 1587." Mace was supplied with a copy of Hariot's *A briefe and true report of the new found land of Virginia*, printed in 1588, from which he was told to collect "merchantable commodities" which included sassafras, thought to be a cure for syphilis, as well as "Sweet Gummes of diuers kinds, and many other Apothecary drugges." During the early journeys, someone had taken careful notes on the Native's language and Mace was given a copy of that lexicon so that he could communicate with the local people.

Mace's 1602 journey from Weymouth to the New World was only five months long, though it appears it was meant to be much longer given the supplies that were loaded onto the ship he commanded. Weather forced him to leave before he had filled his ship with the expensive plants he was there for, but the cargo that did make it back to Weymouth was sold to German apothecaries; unfortunately, the goods he held back as payment for his services were confiscated by one of Elizabeth's ministers, who disliked Raleigh and punished Mace because of his association with the controversial privateer.

It is also those supplies which provide more evidence that that journey was not intended to find the missing colonists; Mace's barke was loaded with tools for digging up plants and for setting up a long term camp, not with the kinds of things, farming equipment, building materials, and so forth, a group of Europeans would need to live forever at Roanoke.

After this last Raleigh-sponsored journey, Mace disappears from the historic record. Not long after, Sir Walter was put in the tower in 1603 by James I, just one year after Elizabeth's death.

Pyrotes and "their roads, haunts, creeks, and maintainers"

The Dorset coast was a perfect haunt for pirates, who found the many small bays, craggy shores, and often-cooperative residents the perfect combination to support their "businesses." They brought the booty they had stolen from ships along the coast and with the help of their many collaborators, made a great deal of money from their illegal, often violent, efforts. But who were these men?

Famous people like local Sir Walter Raleigh are often referred to as pirates because of the incredible wealth they gained for themselves and their queen through capture of ships belonging to foreign powers, usually those at war with England. But technically, Raleigh and others like him were not pirates, they were privateers. The difference was that privateers held "letters of Marque," which were licenses granted by Queen Elizabeth permitting Raleigh and his peers to plunder on her behalf. Some might argue that privateer is just a polite term for queen's pirates, but there was a difference.

"Real" pirates were men – and some women – working around the English coastline, plundering at will. The Dorset coast had been a favourite pirate haunt for centuries, making life dangerous for local fishermen, mariners, shippers, merchants and those living along the coast. Some of those pirates had a lot of help from the locals, especially in Weymouth, Melcombe, Portland and their neighbouring villages.

This Ancient pirate Callis, who most refreshed himself upon the Coast of Wales, who grew famous, till Queene Elizabeth of Blessed Memory, hanged him... Captain John Smith writing about Captain John Callis

Piracy was not unique to Queen Elizabeth's reign. Her grandfather Henry VII and her father, Henry VIII, had been plagued by complaints from coastal communities around the country, all worried about being vulnerable to pirate attacks. Local maps drawn during Henry VII's reign depicted gibbets running from Jordan Hill in Preston all along the Purbeck, where pirates were hung when caught by local officials. But a royal proclamation issued in 1580 indicated that, hangings or no, the problem had become endemic during the Elizabethan era. It stated that pirates 'at this day commit more spoils and robberies on all sides than have been heard of in former times.'

In Dorset, the pirates made their ways from Studland Bay to Portland, leading one local official in 1582 to complain that they swarmed along this coast, and 'the common infamy of this poor island and me...the place of their repair is here where in truth they are my masters...and when they choose to come to land, they are so strong and well-appointed as they cannot be on the sudden repulsed.'

Part of the reason for the increase was the new-found wealth brought in by the discovery of Newfoundland, now part of Canada. Dorset fishermen were able to catch incredible amounts of fish along that North American coast line, bringing their loads home to sell here and in Europe. This meant an increase in shipping traffic, all adding to the attraction of this area to pirates.

Three of the most famous of those Elizabethan pirates were John Callis, Robert Hicks and "Captain" Court. Their stories help to explain why Weymouth and surrounds were their favourite haunts. Though Callis was Welsh, he spent a great deal of time in Dorset, where in both Bridport and Lulworth he had "friends" who were happy to hide him when he came ashore.

In 1577, coastal commissioners who were not locals were appointed to investigate just who was making life so easy for Callis, Court and Hicks. This was a part of one of many attempts to crack down on pirates around the country; the move included a law that enabled officials to prosecute and fine anyone found helping pirates, as well as allowing local officials to issue licences to anyone who wanted to "pirate hunt."

Fishery trades - In *Discourse and Discovery of the Newfoundland* (1620) by Richard Whitbourne, the author lists some of the goods made and sold locally to the fishermen who worked the Newfoundland fisheries. These included nets, hooks, leads, lines, rope, bread, and beer. Bakers, brewers, coopers, chandlers, net-makers, tackle-makers, smiths, hook-makers, carpenters, and rope-makers were among the many Weymouth and neighbouring tradesmen who supplied the fishermen, though they may not have realised just how important their work was to the international trade.

One of the first problems this commission encountered was finding jury members who could be appointed to serve at captured pirates' trials; everyone in the local community seemed to have some kind of connection to the men. When questioned, many potential jurors admitted to being dealers for the pirates. In Weymouth, Melcombe and their adjoining villages, it was found that there were twenty-one 'chief boatmen' who moved the illegal goods from ship to shore. There were also carriers with carts for hauling the stolen goods, and seventy-five others who were buying from the pirates or selling their goods for them. These helpers even included some of the social elite of the area; when Court's ship was grounded, Sir Richard Rogers of West Lulworth, whose job it was to arrest pirates, instead helped Court get back out to the harbour. He was most likely the "friend" who hid Callis when he needed to elude the other authorities.

Judging by that royal proclamation of 1580, the findings of the commission and the worries of the local officials did not do anything to chase away the pesky pirates, though the most notorious of the local sea villains, John Callis, was eventually caught; even that did not stop him from trying to get free, though. Callis wrote a letter to Lord Walsyngham telling him that if he would release the pirate, he would help rid this coast of piracy by identifying the culprits' "roads, haunts, creeks, and maintainers." It did not work and he was hung in 1602.

Those other pirates!

When James I took the throne, his reign saw a new threat emerge with the appearance of Barbary pirates, sometimes called Corsairs, coming from North Africa. These men represented a much more menacing threat to local people than British, Irish or French pirates, as they not only raided merchant shippers going in and out of Weymouth and other local harbours, they also raided villages and towns, ransacking and kidnapping as they went. Weymouth, Lyme, Poole and other smaller communities lost their men and boys, who were often enslaved and used as oarsmen. The men who survived were sold as white slaves in North African cities. The captured women and girls were also sold as slaves and became house servants or members of the harems of wealthy men.

The problem of foreign pirates became so acute that the leaders of Weymouth complained to London officials in 1622 that the Barbary pirates were causing the town to fall into economic ruin because of the disruption to trade and fishing. It was not until the 19th century, however, that the pirate menace was eliminated, helped in part by the American government, whose trade was also hurt by the activity, beginning an all-out war against the North Africans.

The total number of English captured by the Barbary pirates between 1600 and 1800 is estimated from anywhere between 100,000 and over a million people.

A dour king

At her death in 1603, Queen Elizabeth's nephew became James I of England and James VI of Scotland. He was a controversial ruler, especially when it came to religion; he was a practicing Catholic in a staunchly Protestant nation. James was also a dour man, with little sense of humour. He imposed restrictions on the British public that were not appreciated, to include making having a drink on a Sunday illegal. And, like kings before him, his reign was an expensive one. At the time of his death, Great Britain was suffering from inflation, continued struggles with its European neighbours, and excessive taxation. On the other hand, this was also a very exciting time for the continued exploration of the New World. And Dorset played an important part in all of it.

Fast Day – During James' rule, if anyone was caught drinking alcohol on a Sunday they were "presented " for " beareing of burthens on the Saboath Day." When a Weymouth constable was found to be so drunk that "hee could nether goe nor stand" local authorities imposed a Fast Day on the entire community for the constable's sins.

'The 4th May of two men which brought herrings and laded awey certain Newlonde fyshe…'

Before and after Sir Walter Raleigh's death, Dorset men continued to play important roles in the explorations that extended British influence around the world. In May 1583 another of Elizabeth's favourite courtiers, Sir Humphrey Gilbert, sailed from Weymouth on his ship the Delight, with Weymouth native Captain Richard Clark at the helm. They were off to explore, and try to get rich, in the New World. Although Weymouth fishermen had been sailing there to benefit from the huge numbers of fish they were able to catch, it was Gilbert and Clark who claimed the rich fishing grounds off Newfoundland for the Crown.

After staking that claim, it became pivotal to the economy of the West Country, especially for Dorset, where fishing boats from Weymouth, Melcombe Regis and other small communities sailed back and forth across the Atlantic for many years.

The Black Dog – An old pub in Weymouth helps commemorate the importance of Newfoundland to local history; its name was changed to the Black Dog to celebrate the arrival in Britain of a dog breed new to the English: the Newfoundland. The owner of the pub is said to have been the first English owner of the breed, the puppy arriving on one of the fishing boats coming in to Weymouth Harbour.

Erecting a new Pier...

The local economy also experienced a boost when James I commissioned a banqueting hall to be added to Whitehall Palace in 1619. It was designed by one of England's most important architects, Inigo Jones, and constructed of Portland stone. Jones and his assistant spent a great deal of time on Portland, surveying the crown lands for just the right kind of limestone. The project was so important to the king that it included building a new pier at Portland harbour, just to load the stones onto the ships. Those travelled along the Purbeck coast and up to London, where they were pulled up the Thames and unloaded near the construction site.

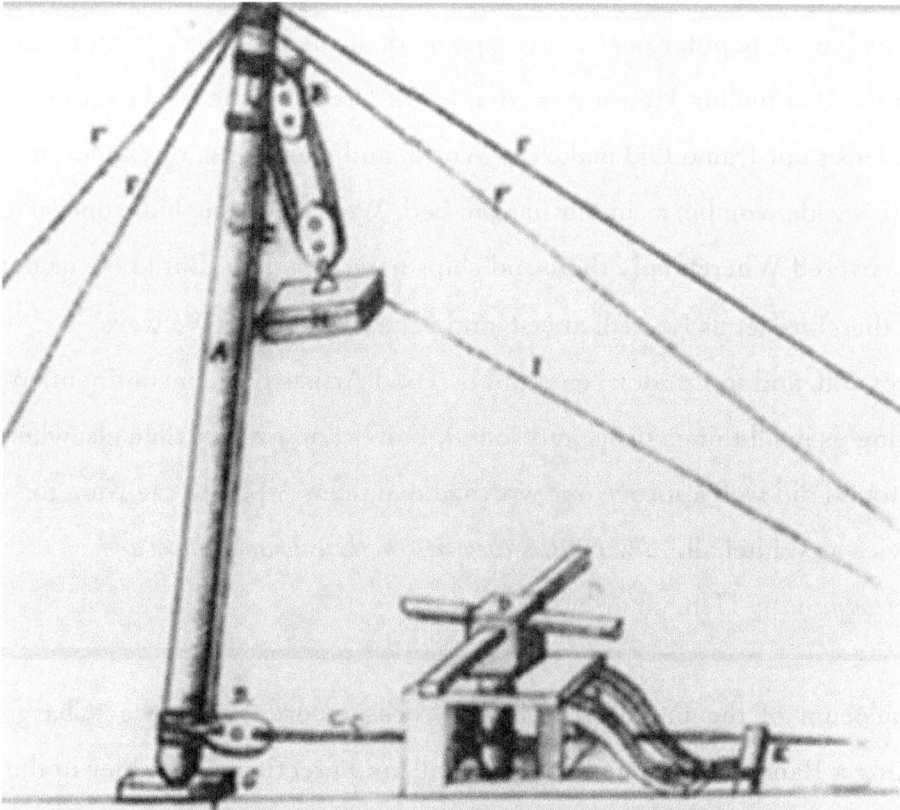

Inigo Jone's Portland Stone Pulley

129

Let us lye - A popular poet wrote a poem dedicated to Portland stone the year the Banqueting House was completed: "ere since the Architect of Heavens's fair frame Did make the World, and man to use the same; In Earth's wide wombe, as in our nat'rall bed, We have beene hid, conceal'd, and covered,Where many thousand ships have sailed by..But knew us not, and therefore let us lye, Till at last, and very lately too. . .We were discover'd, and to London sent, and by good Artists tryde incontinent; Who finding us in all things firme and sound, Fairer and greater than elsewhere are found did well approve our worth above them All Unto the King for Service at Whitehall." *Their Birth, their Mirth, their Thankfulness and Advertisement* by Henry Farley, 1622

The account of the Paymaster of the Works recorded that the "Charges in building a Banqueting House at Whitehall, and erecting a new Pier in the Isle of Portland, for conveyance of stone from thence to Whitehall" were £15,648 3s; that included £712 19s for the pier and £14,940 4s for the hall itself.

The Royal Scaffold - The "Banqueting House" was finished on the 31st of March 1622, but the crown did not pay for it until 1633, eight years after James I had died. It was his son, Charles I, who paid for the Portland stone; ironically, when Charles was put to death by Parliamentarian Oliver Cromwell, his scaffold was placed against the wall of the grand banqueting hall his father had built and he had paid for.

Inigo Jones' St. Paul's Cathedral

The Fleet from Abbotsbury

THE REVEREND MR. WHITE

The Rev. Mr. White, Minister of Dorchester, encouraged by the success of Plymouth Colony, projected the New Settlement in Massachusetts Bay.

The History of New England, 1719

The most recognisable ship in American history is The Mayflower, which carried the first English religious dissenters, the Pilgrims, to the New World. Although the ship departed from Plymouth in 1620 on that momentous journey, the Mayflower had been a familiar site in Weymouth harbour since at least the 1590s, hauling cargoes of cloth, canvas, and wine up and down the southern coast, from Southampton to Wales and back. By the time this small cargo ship arrived to pick up its human cargo in 1620, it was quite an old vessel, but still had other important journeys to make.

Another group of dissenters followed the Pilgrims a decade later, led

133

by the Reverend John Hull from Crewkerne, Somerset. Like the Pilgrims, Hull was seeking the freedom to worship according to his own beliefs, beliefs that did not always mesh with those of the Church of England. He recruited individuals and families from Somerset and Dorset, and according to Dorset County records, in the summer of 1634 "there went out to New England 20 ships, with 2000 planters." This group included farmers from Weymouth, Broadwey, and Batcombe.

The following year, after landing in Boston and moving south of that town, the Reverend Hull and his followers, 100 people from 21 different local families, were joined by another smaller group already living there. In 1635 they named their community "Weymouth." Weymouth, Massachusetts was and still is a thriving community, and was the birth place of Abigail Adams, the wife of the second American president, John Adams. Another group of dissenters left from the harbour in 1640, but this one was even bigger with 900 Dorset residents, 150 of them from Weymouth.

Massachusetts was also the destination of another Dorset religious community who were members of dissenting churches. The Reverend John White, a rector from Dorchester and a supporter of the Pilgrims, established the Dorchester Company, a business that tried to raise money by shipping and selling fish from the New World to help the non-conformist community. The business was a failure, but with the help of another Dorchester man, White tried again and founded the Massachusetts Bay Company which made its money from shipping people to the New World instead of fish to Dorset.

This company was a success and chartered Weymouth boats to send local Puritans - though White supported them, he did not consider himself a Puritan - to Massachusetts. The Amity left Weymouth harbour in 1625, the Abigail left in 1628; the community these Puritans established in the New World became known as Dorchester. And the man who helped found the company that paid for much of this effort? He also sailed to Massachusetts on the Abigail. His name was John Endicott and he became the very first governor of that colony.

Charles I

When King James I died, his son became Charles I. It was during his time as king that some of the worst conflicts on English soil since the time of the early Anglo-Saxons took place.

The young king, who was only twenty-four when he took the throne, inherited his father's role in the long struggle being fought between various European countries, historically known as the Thirty Years War. But Charles tried and failed to meet his commitments to the war; both of his own attempts to send expeditions to France and Spain failed. He also married a Catholic, the daughter of French King Henry IV, which worried many Englishmen. No one wanted his children to be raised Catholic, because it could lead to the same kind of terrible religious conflict experienced in the previous century. Charles' greatest problems arose, however, when he, like his father, could not agree with Parliament on issues regarding how to run the country.

From 1625 to 1629, the king and many Parliamentarians argued about everything, especially taxation. Charles wanted to impose higher and higher taxes, some of which hit the local community hard - especially the Ship Money tariff - to fund his wars and his public building works, but Parliament refused. The King's response was the same as his father's had been: he locked the Parliamentarians out of Westminster. The stalemate lasted for eleven years.

A busy port...

Early on in Charles' reign, Weymouth was a bustling though often troubled town, filled with merchants, ship owners, shipwrights, sailors, as well as tradespeople and transients. In 1628 alone, it had 176 registered sailors; Melcombe Regis, 111. This was more than a quarter of the total of all sailors in Dorset and represented a tremendous increase over prior years, explained by the fact that in that year alone, there were many new ships based in Weymouth harbour: at least 26. Other Dorset ports did not have anything like this kind of traffic: Lyme Regis, for instance, had 18 ships, while Bridport, Charmouth and Chideock did not have one between them. But the cost of maintaining a port that could support all these vessels and the trade they represented was not all good news, in fact it took a real toll on the community budget, because the town of Weymouth and its ships' owners bore the entire cost.

Alewives - The local alewives, those women who brewed and sold beer, had been important members of the community since the Middle Ages, but during Charles I's reign, the authorities declared it illegal for women to brew ale. The women brewers were told they had to buy the ale they sold from male brewers. The trouble was that these were independent business women and were not particularly interested in what the male authorities had to say; they carried on brewing and selling, challenging local officials to enforce the law. It appears the alewives won.

Once a ship entered the harbour, to use the port facilities, its captain had to pay four pence (4d) for each tonne of anchorage. That charge went to funding the cranes the town provided for loading and unloading ships' cargoes; the maintenance of the Petty Customs house; the wood for the fires that heated harbour buildings during the winter; and workers' salaries, as well as paying the expenses incurred on maintaining the wharf and repairing the barrows, wheeled carts that carried smaller goods and supplies on and off ships. The fees, however, were never enough to meet the demands of the upkeep of a busy harbour.

Soap and sailors - The English commitment to the complicated alliances involved in fighting the European Thirty Years War had an impact on the local community in a number of ways, some of them stranger than others. To include on soap manufacture. The Dorset soap industry had been thriving for centuries, and by the 17th century, many Britons considered soap a necessity, so much so that it was often part of the shipments of goods to the New World. Household soap was produced locally because of the availability of lanolin from Dorset sheep; it was of such high quality, Dorset soap was even known to the king, or at least his tax men, who when looking for creative ways to raise taxes to fight in Europe, decided to put a special duty on that local industry, a move that was not welcomed by those involved in its production.

As in other eras, the fear of French attack was alive and well in the first half of the 17th century, especially over the very real threat of raids on merchant ships. Local officials knew they needed to increase the defensive capability of the harbour, but over the years, Sandsfoot Castle had been allowed to deteriorate and Portland Castle was not prepared for serious defence either. To bolster harbour security, merchants and ship owners paid for two new blockhouses, one at Melcombe, the other on the Nothe. They were built in 1625 and 1626 and both were armed.

Sandsfoot Castle Ruins

Adding to that financial burden, the king's taxes also had to be paid; in January 1627, Weymouth Mayor Thomas Lokier noted that local ship owners objected to the king's financial demands and he hired a courier to deliver a letter to Charles on behalf of the owners. It explained why they could not pay: "…their Lordships have revived an order of last summer for the towns of Weymouth and Poole to set forth two ships for the King's Service the writers allege that their inability has since that time much increased, as well be made to appear by a person whom as directed they have employed to appear for them before the Council."

The letter does not appear to have had the desired effect, given that two months later the King's Council authorised the impressment of ships, a vital source of funds for the community, from Weymouth and four other coastal towns, empowering the Duke of Buckingham and his associates to enforce the order. The letter may not have helped, but it seems that one owner did, successfully, stand up against impressment: Weymouth's Henry Cuttance, who owned the Gift of God and the Flower, questioned the authority of the Duke and this in turn encouraged the local men who had been impressed to sail on Cuttance's ships to run away, escaping into the surrounding countryside.

Young Sailors

The problem of impressment persisted for another two hundred years at least, though there were those who continued to fight such demands; in 1636, for instance, a King's man called Robert Newman came to impress Weymouth shipwrights to work in the king's ship yard in Woolwich. Mayor Thomas Ledoze stepped in this time and managed to prevent the impressment of a single man.

With the exception of Portland

During Charles I's reign, there was a great deal of civic building taking place, and Portland stone was a vital component, especially in the St. Paul's Cathedral renovations. The local stone works were so important to the royal building plans that it was decreed the only sailors who were immune to official impressment were those who worked on the ships carrying Portland stone destined for the King's projects; as early as 1628, the crew of the Weymouth ship the Mayflower were officially declared exempt from any kind of impressment.

This continued into the 1630s, as Inigo Jones, Charles I's choice of architects for the project, travelled to Portland to supervise the quarrying for the repair of St. Paul's.

The French Threat...

The complicated politics of the European Thirty Years War led to increased tension between the English and the French...again. This made merchant ships vulnerable to French attack in the Channel, but the on and off again nature of the war meant that English manufacturers and merchants and their ships were still involved in the import-export businesses between the two countries. When the conflict heated up, English ships were in danger of being embargoed upon arrival in French ports, while others vanished, never to be heard from again.

In 1627 and 1628, seven Weymouth ships were embargoed as they tried to deliver English goods to French ports. Far more dramatic was the 1628 report to the King's Council which documented a much bigger loss to the community: 87 ships, worth a total of £100,000, along with 1,160 crew members had "disappeared." To be fair, though the French were often blamed for this catastrophic loss, it is not clear if it was the French blockading the Western ports, or increased pirate activity in the Channel. It was likely to have been a combination of the two.

Other famous buildings made from Portland stone – Other important structures built of Portland stone include: New Scotland Yard, the Victoria and Albert Museum, the Cenotaph, Waterloo Bridge, the Greenwich Royal Naval College, the National Gallery, the Northern Ireland Parliament Building and the United Nations Headquarters in New York. Many of London's finest churches are also made from the world-famous stone.

The number of merchants and ship owners using the Weymouth port facilities in the 17th century was tremendous. In 1637 alone, an incomplete list included 141 men and two women with shares in the cargo coming and going from Weymouth. The bulk of those cargoes was not owned by Weymouth residents, however; most belonged to the better off inland merchants, many of them from Dorchester. This lack of local wealth was demonstrated by a letter sent five years earlier. In 1632, the mayor of Weymouth had sent a message to the King's Council explaining why the town's merchants could not attend a meeting about trade with that council because 'the merchants of that town being but four that trade with France, being so few in number of mean abilities (the greatest merchants that traffic through that port living in inland towns) made excuses...'

Coal, Treager, Treguier, and Poldavis

Clearly all the local and inland merchants were not of "mean abilities" however. The goods being imported and exported through Weymouth's port were incredibly varied and certainly tell a great deal about not just what was being shipped, but about the industry of Dorset and its trading partner regions and nations. One of the newer imports into Weymouth, much of which was repackaged and sent inland into neighbouring communities, was coal. Most of it came from the new mines of Newcastle and Sunderland, as well as Barry in Wales.

Other cargo arriving into Weymouth from Breton and Normandy, for instance, included a variety of cloth. These had wonderful names like Dowlis and Treager, which came from Treguier in Brittany, and both were course linens. Another, Poldavis, was a rough sail cloth, which must have competed with the locally made varieties, or indicate the local weavers could not keep up with demand. There were also fine linens used to make table cloths and serviettes as well as thread. Wools, flax and hemp from Spain and Ireland arrived in quantity, as did huge amounts of chicken feathers and writing paper, both from a variety of countries. Even cargoes of playing cards were shipped into the local port.

Wood and marine stores - masts, small spars, clapboards, cordage - were shipped in to Weymouth, along with cod and herring nets, building materials, plaster, pitch and tar. There were also dyes that were used to colour both imported and locally woven cloth: indigo and woad were popular blue dyes and powdered red madder made beautiful dark red shades.

Irish merchants exported beef, pork, bacon, butter, cheese, herring, wheat, tallow, and hides into Weymouth; the French sent prunes, figs, raisins, currants, almonds and walnuts; and cochineal, another dye that turned cloth a brilliant scarlet red, along with spices from Asia like mace, licorice and ginger. Spanish wines were very popular here, as well as 'acquavite' and vinegar. The Bretons sent soap, turpentine, sugar, molasses and salt: there were 21 loads of salt in 1634 alone, and this is another of the cargoes that is a bit puzzling, given Portland had a thriving salt industry.

Onions and oranges…

Two interesting cargoes from Bordeaux in the same year are worth a note. One was imported by Weymouth's Gregory Babbidge and Company on the Hopewell and it contained nine tonnes of Burgundy wine, prunes, feathers, pitch, 1,507 cases of oranges, 50 ropes of onions and numerous bags of nuts. The following month, Weymouth merchant Henry Russell's men unloaded wine, vinegar, pitch, wheat, feathers, nuts and prunes from the Willing Mind. People living in and around Weymouth seemed to love their wine and fruits.

There were also huge cargoes coming in from London, where big merchants bought in bulk and sold the goods in lots to merchants from other parts of the country. These included items like fabrics, ribbons, pots and glassware, "grocery ware," guns, cast iron shot, gunpowder, muskets, pikes, swords, bandoliers <leather belts that held ammunition>, iron shot and lead shot. Sugar was also an important import that found its way in huge quantities to Weymouth.

Dorset Kersies

There was a real shift in diet in the 17th century, especially in what people drank. Although coffee, cocoa and tea were a huge hit for those who could afford them, Weymouth was not a major recipient of those exports, but it was for sugar. Without that precious commodity, the harsh varieties of coffee, cocoa and tea consumed during this time would have been too bitter to drink. Sugar was also an example of the kind of product brought into port by local merchants, only to be repackaged and reshipped to other ports around the UK, all ready to be purchased by individual consumers.

And what was leaving from Weymouth? Seventeenth century Dorset manufacturers exported cloth, to include Dorset Kersies, Barnstable bays, crested and uncrested sarums, small and broad cloth, plain dunsters, canton cottons, and Chard Kersies, making cloth about sixty percent of any given cargo leaving the harbour. There was also plenty of fish, to include dried Newfoundland varieties, as well as hides, hops, lead, salt, and wood. Then there were the shipments to the New World.

In 1625, a company owned by a local Member of Parliament, Sir Walter Erle sent what appears to be multiple charitable shipments to the "Christians planted in New England." These included meal, malt, and cattle. Other loads sent to planters in "Matachusset-New England" included butter, peas, grits, cheese, salt, bread, beef, fish, oil, butter, soap, clothes, stockings, boots, shoes, hats, nails, and calve skins, as well as "divers sortes of household stuffe, apparrell and other provisions for the necessary use of themselves, their wives, children and servants. All wich provisions are valued as they cost and are wirth heere and are allowed to go free custome." The generous contribution is a clue to the history of North American immigration, as locals who had left for a new life clearly needed their friends and families back home to keep them clothed and fed well into the 17th century.

The immigrants may have benefitted from the waving of "custome," meaning the export tax paid by merchants and shippers to the king, but the local community, for all the bustle and trade, continued to struggle to maintain the infrastructure necessary to maintain that vibrancy. In 1628, only a year after the last time they had protested paying taxes, town leaders sent a petition to the Duke of Buckingham explaining why they were struggling: "these towns (Weymouth and Melcombe Regis) are so seated that 200 ships of any burthen may ride there and land at all times without tide. They are much decayed for they and the Town of Dorchester yielded the King £5,000 p.a. in customs."

Thence removed…

As early as 1620, then-Weymouth's mayor John Bond suggested to the king's Council that because the inland merchants were making most of the profit from imports and exports, and did not have to pay the customs' duties, Weymouth should be allowed to charge them a port tax. Those merchants' answer was to remove their business to Poole, or as the mayor put it 'inland merchants who were accustomed to trade thence have removed their trade to Poole to avoid the duty.'

The same year, the mayor complained about the fact that local ship owners had lost £3000 at sea in the prior years because of seizures by 'Algerine' (Algerian) pirates. The town leaders' answer was to outfit Weymouth's own man-of-war (war ship), but that was so expensive they had to borrow the money which they could not afford to repay. Two years later, the mayor asked for volunteer contributions and when small amounts trickled in, instead of being unhappy with the amount he collected, he expressed surprise because the small amount 'is large considering how their trade is depressed by losses from Turkish pirates who have attacked and taken almost every bark sent last year from Spain and Gibraltar and have caused such a damp on trade that instead of 39 ships only 11 have gone this year to Newfoundland.' In 1627 alone, £26,000 in losses were attributed to pirates, and this figure did not include the cost of helping the wives and children of the sailors who were enslaved.

Although there were other calls to provide armed ships to accompany the Weymouth vessels to and fro, the idea was dismissed as disrespectful to the king and his navy, even though the king's forces were not helping the local community with the problem. More telling is that many also felt the reason pirates were attracted to Weymouth itself was because so many locals traded with them. The same old story.

Strong and nimble

By 1632, Spanish pirates were also preying on ships plying the southwest waters. One of the pirate ships was captured just outside of Weymouth harbour, but that did not stop others from not just terrorising merchant ships, the pirates actually landed and pillaged local communities. It was so bad at one point that merchants and ship owners petitioned the King's Council, describing another foreign threat, 'the pirates of Sallee <North Western Morocco> becoming so numerous, strong and nimble in their ships and are so well piloted into these channels by English and Irish captives (of whom they retain almost 2,000 in slavery)…that the petitioners dare not send out their ships…pray speedy course for securing trade, suppressing these pirates and obtaining the freedom of those in captivity.'

Waymouth Ffarthying

During the years between the reigns of Elizabeth I and Charles II, there was a shortage of national small coinage, the sort exchanged between local merchants and their customers. That and the fact that banks were privately owned and used by the middle classes and the wealthy, there were few facilities to act as "clearing houses" for basic coinage, as opposed to gold coinage and script, for instance.

Bristol was the first town on record to petition the queen, in 1594, for the right to mint coins for use in community stores, pubs and inns, but other towns followed suit – without applying for permission – and Weymouth began minting its own coinage by the early 17th century. The coins were made out of a variety of base metals, to include copper, brass and tin and were minted by local business people. They had the names and addresses of the men and women who had them made, some with the date of issue also stamped on them. These included "James Budd of Weymouth in Dorset from 1666"; "Bartholomew Beer in Waymouth, 1658"; "James Stanly in Waymouth, 1664"; "Francis Regis"; and "Thomas Hide, Waymouth and Melcombe Regis."

The town leadership also got into the coinage act by minting the "Waymouth Ffarthying." At a town meeting, "Att a full Hall held on Friday, the fifth daye of Novembre, 1669," those leaders declared that "Alsoe yt ys agreede uppon, Thatt Mister Deputie Maior bee pleased to laie outt Tenn pounds in ffarthynges, for the Townes use and profitt of the Poore, the superscription on the one side to be 'A 'Waymouth Ffarthyng', and on the other syde For the Poore, with the Towne Armes." They also issued another with "A Weymouth Farthing for the Poor, 1669," stamped on one side, "The Town Arms" on the other.

A Weymouth Farthing

In 1672, Charles II wanted to keep a tighter hold over the national monetary system and declared local minting illegal; he ordered the national provision of small coinage, but it was a very important part of the economic life of many local economies up to that point.

Public Works of the times

Although history tends to point the finger at the Tudors for ever-increasing persecution of the poorest sector of society, as the years passed, it did not get much better under the Stuarts. The Weymouth town accounts of 1620 recorded the purchase of "Flax is to be bought with £20 of the poorestock to sett the poore on worck," with "Four Overseers of Poor" appointed to be sure the material was put to good use.

Three years later, town leaders came up with a plan to buy a home, yet again "for the settings of the poore at worcke." They intended to hire a woman to keep "the poor children at work, and for apprenticing or employing them." Many of those children worked at "Twenty frames for "ynckle," which were for the "making were to be got," and "Benj. White's wife" was "to be mistress" of the young labourers. Ynckle, or inckle, was the fabric introduced by Dutch weavers, used for making belts, straps and trims, and produced on small, boxy looms. Those were worked with an up and down motion rather than side to side, meaning many children could be squashed into a small space to perform the labour. The site of this workhouse was built over the Tudor poor house, and later, the 19th century workhouse was built on the same piece of land.

Crossing at Smallmouth Bay

THE AFFIDAVIT OF ALLAN MARISELY

The Affidavit of Allan Manisley of London, Gent. Who made oath that there lieth of the South Side of Weymouth a Creeke called the Fleete which hath always been accounted as sea lying always under salt water and the Tide there always flowing, the Beach lying South from this Fleet, between it and the South Sea, this Ground being by estimation worth Fourpence an acre or thereabouts and containeth Three thousand acreas as he verily believeth.

For reasons that seem a bit baffling to the 21st century mind, a group of wealthy men from Dorset and Somerset decided that draining the Fleet, the fresh water lagoon that runs parallel to Lyme Bay from Abbotsbury to Weymouth, was a good idea. They believed it would create about 3,000 acres of arable land, a valuable commodity at the time. With the agreement, but no monetary investment on his part, the owner of the land along the Fleet, Sir

John Strangways, agreed to support the scheme. Although the records are not completely clear, visitors to the site - it became quite a tourist Mecca, as newspapers around the country reported on this huge project - recorded what was happening: "This indraught which cometh about by the Easter[n] end of Portland was in hand to bee dreyned to make Pasture Land, whereon was spent great sommes of money in makeinge of sluces, trenches, etts. Inventions to keepe the Tide from comeing in, as also to lett out what is within."

It must have required a huge work force to complete, but the Fleet was drained successfully, only to be refilled during a huge storm in 1632, meaning they had to start all over again. This, however, was not known by a courtier and groom of the King's Bedchamber, George Kirke, who when he found out about the scheme, thought he could make some money by proving that the Fleet was part of the sea, making it royal land rather than the property of Strangways.' He offered to help broker a deal between the schemers and the king, with a nice piece of the land or cash in return for the "royal favour." But, when Kirke found out that the Fleet was not drained, he was so angry – he was convinced that the project had been sabotaged, not that stormy weather was the culprit – he began a legal case against the schemers. When they proved they had not re-flooded the lagoon, Kirke decided to sign on with Strangways himself, that way keeping all the land, or the profit from it, for just the two of them.

'...Sir John Strangways and his heires shall have in part of his or their three parts, all that part or parcel of the said Fleete lying adjoining being or abbuting upon the Manor of Abbotsbury so far as the Brook which devideth the Manor of Abbotsbury and Langton containing by estimation Two hundred acres or Thereabouts (be it more or less).'

Eventually Kirke seems to have realised that this was not a practical project and he gave up and signed the rights to the Fleet over to Strangways, who had to pay ten pounds a year for that privilege. It remains in that family, as part of the Ilchester estate, today.

The Fleet

The Civil War

Over the years of tension between the king and Parliament, the country began to divide into two groups, one that supported the monarchy as an absolute power, the other that wanted an independent Parliament that had an equal share of power with the monarch. Charles became so angry with a handful of Parliamentarians for their public criticisms of his rule that he ordered their arrest. Even he seems to have realised that this was a step too far, but it was too late; furious fighting broke out between the two factions. That conflict, which is actually a series of three conflicts beginning in 1642, is simply referred to as the English Civil War.

Locally, the Royalists and Parliamentarians made life very difficult for all. Towns and villages declared their allegiances; Melcombe Regis, along with Dorchester, declared for Parliament and Weymouth and Portland supported the monarchy. By 1643, it appeared the Royalists were winning control of Dorset, but by the second half of that year, the Parliamentarians were on the rise, when their army advanced from the East and took decisive possession of Dorchester and Weymouth. This was such an important turnaround that Charles headed his army straight to Dorset. After that, both sides battled to take control, winning and losing in turns over a period of years.

The leader of the Parliamentarians - When the conflict between those who supported the king and those who supported parliament began, no clear leadership arose until a Member of Parliament, Oliver Cromwell, a staunch religious reformer and distant relative of Henry VIII's Thomas Cromwell, proved himself a born leader. When he joined the Parliamentary army, Cromwell very quickly made his way up the ranks, eventually turning the unprofessional men who made up the parliamentary army into what became the New Model Army. Cromwell's extreme dedication to Puritanism meant he wanted to see the end of the Stuart line and when he was made Lord Protector of England, something akin to prime minister, he was responsible for seeing Charles I hanged for offences against his realm.

Eventually, it all began to slip away from the Royalists and Charles found himself grasping at straws; he attempted, for instance, to join Cornwall, Devon, Somerset, and Dorset into "Associated Counties" intended to work together to fight for the royal cause. This never happened, however, as it became apparent that the residents of these counties were too different – too independent – to work cooperatively. Contemporaries blamed their differences on "The hilly character of the districts chosen, and their deep inlets of the sea" which "hindered alike easy communication and the growth of a common principle and sentiments."

In February, 1644, Royalist Sir Walter Hastings, governor of Portland, seized one of Weymouth's forts, and then the town itself. Meanwhile, the Parliamentarians hunkered down in Melcombe; they were quickly reinforced with 3,000 horsemen and 1,500 foot soldiers and artillerymen from other parts of the county. The Royalists lost their hold on the local communities and were forced back to Dorchester, with a heavy loss of life. That is when Cromwell himself decided to move his army to the West in hopes of taking advantage of the failing Royalists' cause. When he arrived at Corfe Castle, he "conceived the place might shortly be reduced." But before he destroyed Corfe, Cromwell realised that there was something that needed his attention even more than crushing the remaining Royalist strong holds.

Enter the Clubmen.

Who were the Clubmen? - The professions of most Clubmen indicate that this really was a fight for local survival, not a fight about who would rule. They included Dorset bakers, coopers, gardeners, husbandmen, tailors, millers, tapsters, and warreners, tradesmen whose livelihoods had been hurt or even destroyed by the ongoing struggles for power.

If you offer to plunder, or take our cattel, Be assured we will bid you battle.

Where ever armies march and where ever they fight means death and destruction to the people living there. The English Civil War was no different. Soldiers helped themselves to anything and everything: crops, sheep, cattle, horses, carts and carriages. Locally, Dorset farmers, dairymen and others suffered terrible losses as troops from both sides took whatever they could carry. Anger over the impact on their local communities, especially in the West, meant that no matter what their original sentiments - Royalist or Parliamentary - there were many men who banded together to try to stop the war all together. They called themselves the Clubmen, after the primitive weapons some of them carried.

The local Clubmen were fed up with the way in which Weymouth, Melcombe and other local towns and villages kept changing hands, and the devastating effects the battles had on their lives. They petitioned the king to allow them to take over the garrisons of Dorset and Wiltshire, hoping to act as a catalyst for peace until both sides could come to some agreement. This included taking over the forts of Weymouth and Portland. What happened instead is the Clubmen became a third faction in the war, arming themselves and marching on various towns in Dorset. When Cromwell's army arrived in Dorchester, Colonel Sydenham, the governor of Weymouth, warned of the danger from "these club risers, who were there to stop that army."

By mid-summer of 1645, Parliamentarians were so strong that they had only three things left to achieve to control all of Dorset: take Sherborne, destroy Corfe Castle and eliminate the Clubmen.

The biggest battle in Dorset during the Civil War was not Royalist versus Parliamentarian, it was Parliamentarian versus Clubmen. A thousand of Cromwell's soldiers went straight from their win at Sherborne to Hambleton Hill in August of 1645. They came up against somewhere between two and four thousand Clubmen, whose leader was a Reverend Bravell from Compton Abbas; in spite of being hopelessly outnumbered, Cromwell's army routed the Clubmen. Some of those got away, others were killed or captured and imprisoned. After the embarrassing route, Cromwell dismissed the Dorset civilians as "poor silly creatures."

The Navigation Acts...

Not long after the Parliamentarians defeated the Royalists, Cromwell found himself embroiled in another conflict, but this was one of his very own making. In 1652, he demanded tribute for all the herring caught within thirty miles off the English coast. This policy had originated with the Stuarts, but with all the conflict over so many years, it had not been enforced. At the same time, Cromwell passed the Navigation Act which required all goods imported into England had to be carried either on English ships or ships from the same countries the goods were produced; adding insult to injury, he also told other nations that their ships must salute English warships when they passed them in the English Channel. The most offended by these demands, specifically the Act and the salute, were the Dutch, who considered themselves at least the equals of the English when it came to naval and economic power.

In 1653, Dutch warships fired on British naval ships when the Dutch navy was accompanying a Dutch merchant fleet through the Channel. It was an indecisive battle, but it sparked another, more dramatic clash, the Three Day's Battle. This fight is better known as the Battle of Portland because it was fought at the tip of the Isle. Though who won and who lost was not clear cut, the British ships were not badly damaged; the Dutch, on the other hand, lost twelve warships and fifty merchant ships.

The Dutch Anglo War

Admiral of the Blue

William Penn (1621 – 1670) was born in Bristol and went to sea as a young man, eventually becoming a ship's captain in 1642. He served in the Parliamentarian navy during the Civil War and in 1653 was appointed the Admiral of the Blue Division at the Battle of Portland, where he led the fight against the Dutch during the First Anglo-Dutch War. He retired in 1655, but was asked to rejoin the Royal Navy in 1660, the same year he was chosen to bring Charles II home to take his throne. Also in 1660, he was elected to Parliament as an MP for Weymouth. William Penn was the father of the Quaker leader, also William Penn, who founded the American colony of Pennsylvania.

Dancing on his grave

When Oliver Cromwell died in 1658, most Englishmen were not unhappy about his death. He was a very religious man and had imposed laws that made even the simplest pleasures illegal: dancing, drinking, gambling… the average Englishman had missed them terribly and after Cromwell's son, who took over after his death, failed in his attempt to continue as the Lord Protector, they danced the nights away, returned to the theatre and once again celebrated Christmas. Weymouth, though it had many conservative nonconformists, was alive with celebration for months after Cromwell's death: the public houses were back in business.

The White Hart

At the close of the English Civil War, so many sailors and soldiers had died, the navy and army were badly under manned. The shortage was so acute, in 1654 Parliament passed an ordinance making impressment legal. Prior to this, going back at least as far as Edward I, it was the king's right to force men into service, but by passing a formal law allowing any military officer the right to seize men anywhere, anytime, took impressment to a new level.

It had been a problem off and on for many centuries, to include during Charles I's reign, but the new law made all men vulnerable. The process hit harbour towns like Weymouth and Melcombe Regis the hardest. It got so bad, in fact, that groups of men belonging to press gangs, people who made money illegally from impressing men and "selling" them to naval captains who turned a blind eye to the process, gathered at the White Hart tavern in the heart of Weymouth and rioted against the government and its new policy because it was hurting *their* 'business.' This did nothing to stop the navy from taking as many men as possible from the local communities and the threat of impressment was a constant part of life for men and their families living on or near the Dorset coast, even into the 19th century.

> **1649** – The same year Charles I was executed, a group of Royalists from Jersey and France arrived on the Dorset coast in hopes of taking control over Weymouth and Portland for the "use and service" of Charles II. The attempt failed. However, it does bring an unsung local hero, at least to those who supported the Parliamentarian cause, into the story. The commander of Weymouth and Sandsfoot garrisons, Col. John Heane, was angry with the "Jerseymen pirates" for their activities along the Dorset coast and he set out to get rid of the Royalist leadership on Jersey in retaliation. He sailed from Weymouth with ships and soldiers in October 1651 and in spite of terrible weather and thousands of Royalists ready to repulse his efforts, Heane and his fellows chased the local governor to the castle on Jersey, eventually allowing those who survived his invasion to escape to France.

Bring back the royals!

The eldest surviving son of Charles I was born in May in 1630. He was twelve years old when the Civil War had begun and by the age of fourteen, had been made the commander-in-chief of western England, which included Dorset. Because his father did not win the struggle against the Parliamentarians, his son had to flee the country. He made his way to Bridport, trying to find a ship from Weymouth to escape to France, but that became impossible. Instead, the king's son fled to the Netherlands, which is where he heard about his father's execution in 1649, eventually joining his mother who was already in exile at the French court. Her brother was King Louis XIII.

Determined, the eldest son, also named Charles, convinced the Scots to help him retake the throne, but was unable to defeat Cromwell. Then in 1660, after Cromwellian rule had failed to succeed after Cromwell died and his son was unable to carry on in his father's place, the English invited their exiled king to return. The Restoration had begun.

> **Weymouth's tree** – Thomas Thynne, the 1st Viscount of Weymouth in the late 17th and early 18th centuries, is credited with introducing – and naming – a new species of tree to the UK in 1705. It was called the Weymouth Pine. It was actually discovered by a 17th century Weymouth man who had emigrated to what is now the US State of Maine and found the tree, a native to that area. The Weymouth pine was very important to the expanding Royal navy at that time, as it grew tall and straight and was perfect for making ships' masts.

The Politics of Trade in 17th century Weymouth

A large percentage of Weymouth's local councillors were also ship owners and merchants, sometimes both. In some cases, multiple members of the same family served as councillors either concurrently or one generation after the other. One example was Mayor George Pley, who was mayor in 1650, 1658, 1665 and 1669; though he had been an avid supporter of Cromwell, when Charles II was restored to the throne in 1660, Pley used his position in local politics to sell his wares to the new and growing royal navy; his sailcloth could be found on many of the war ships anchored in Weymouth harbour that same year.

Charles II

Although King Charles II (1660 – 1685) had been invited to return to rule the United Kingdom, he was not universally popular, to include in Dorset. This was, in part, because of the many nonconformists living in the county and their concerns over Charles' wife, Spanish princess Catherine of

Braganza, who was a devout Catholic.

Rather than return Britain to Catholic rule though, in 1662, Charles signed the Act of Uniformity, which was created to strengthen the powers of the Church of England and ended up making life quite difficult for those who did not worship in the official church. This was in direct conflict with Cromwell's belief that Britain needed a "Godly Reformation" so that all could live with a "liberty of conscience." He worked to end the often-cruel treatment of prisoners and the poor, for instance, an area that had reflected the darker side of English life for centuries. Along with this Cromwell had believed that all sects of Protestantism had the right to worship as they saw fit, and those groups were not to interfere with others' beliefs. Non-conformists thrived during his time in office.

Charles II's move was all about reversing the Cromwellian philosophy; life may have been very restrained under him, but it had meant that local preachers who had been allowed to preach because Cromwell did not interfere with the flourishing nonconformist movement, would no longer be allowed that freedom. Any nonconformists who were not sanctioned by the Church of England lost their livings, and could be punished for preaching without permission.

This was followed by the Five Mile Act in 1665.

Otherwise known as the Nonconformists Act, "An Act for restraining Non-Conformists from inhabiting in Corporations," the Five Mile Act became part of the English penal codes that were enacted to force conformity in religion, another attempt to boost the power of the Church of England. It made it illegal for any nonconformist minister who had been expelled from a parish from living within a five mile radius of that town. Thousands of preachers were badly hurt by these two laws, to the point where many were arrested under them, to include at least 72 from Dorset.

There was one Weymouth family in particular who suffered terribly from the sting of Charles' rigid treatment of nonconformists, but whose impact on religion is still felt today.

'Pursuit of Knowledge'

Though it is not certain, Bartholomew Westley was probably born in Dorset. He studied divinity at university and, as a nonconformist, preached in Bridport, then later in Charmouth and Catherston. Because of his "radical views" he was ejected from those positions in 1662, but he did continue to work as an itinerant preacher until the Five Mile Act forced him to leave.

Bartholomew's son, John Westley, was born in 1636 in Bridport. John was sent to school in Dorchester and then on to study at Oxford. Also a nonconformist, John was a devout young man and when he moved back to Dorset, he settled in Weymouth, where he joined a "gathered church," a small congregation of people who believed they were surrounded by others who are not redeemable, a belief they shared with the Puritans.

John preached at Melcombe Regis and Radipole, where he formed his own small church. His congregation considered him to be a devout and dedicated man of God. In 1658, he left Weymouth when he was asked to become the pastor of the church at Winterborne Whitchurch. This was quite a step up, as John was approved by Cromwell's Board of Commissioners, which took him from "casual" preacher to recognised minister. In 1660, the same year Charles II became king, John married the daughter of that famous Dorchester minister who helped the Mayflower Puritans reach America, the Reverend John White.

The timing of John's appointment as pastor could not have been worse. The new anti-conformist laws began to be enforced just as he was to take his place in his new church which meant that in 1662 John was arrested and imprisoned for his preaching. Within a few months, thousands of others, to include many in Dorset, were also ejected from their churches and even their homes.

Not long after he was freed from prison, John's son Samuel was born and the family moved to Melcombe Regis. But they found themselves on the move again as they were driven out of town by the authorities who had begun to enforce the Five Mile Act. They were even fined for living in Melcombe. Fortunately for the Wesleys, a nonconformist friend of some means took pity upon the family and provided a home for them in Preston in 1663. John continued to preach where he could, but in 1664 he was stopped from doing any kind of preaching in public by the Conventicle Act, which made it illegal for more than five people who were not members of the Church of England to gather in one place. Even that did not stop him entirely, though, as he preached in private in Preston and its surrounding villages.

Samuel's family was terribly poor because of the treatment of nonconformists, but like his father, he had friends who paid for his education. He was sent to London to train as a "dissenting" preacher, and later he attended Oxford; then in 1688 he was ordained as a deacon and eventually married and moved to Epworth. Samuel's son John Benjamin Wesley (the "t" had been dropped by then) was born there in 1703. This son of a long line of nonconformist preachers became the founder of the Methodist Church.

> Methodos – Methodist comes from the Greek *methodos*, meaning 'pursuit of knowledge.' It was chosen by Wesley as the name of his religious movement based on his time at Oxford, where he helped form the Holy Club, a group of students who read and discussed the bible.

Indulgence

The terrible impact of the religious policies of Charles II's reign did nothing for the king's reputation. In fact, they were so unpopular by 1672 Charles decided to pass the Declaration of Indulgence, which allowed nonconformist ministers to apply for a licence to preach and their meeting houses in an attempt to ease the religious tension his laws had created. Licenses granted to local nonconformists included "George Thorne, Weymouth Congregationalist" to preach "in the house of James Bud" and "Esther Churchey, Weymouth Presbyterian" who was allowed to open her home to any preacher who was licensed to preach.

> **1676** - "At Weymouth a boy of 15, the son of a Nonconformist, was baptized in church, and given the name of Mice, as he was baptized on the day appointed for an annual sermon by Sir Samuel Mico, a benefactor to the town." *From Charles II State Calendar.*

Sir Samuel Mico was a wealthy merchant who traded in the Far East as a member of the East India Company, which brought exotic silks and spices to England. He lived in London, but owned the George Tavern in Weymouth. When he died in 1666, he left the tavern and 500 pounds to the town: the profits were to be spent each year in "the binding out of three poor children apprentices and for the relief of ten poor decayed seamen of the town" who were over sixty and had no other means of support. He funded the purchase of an old Tudor home on Portland where the seamen lived in relative comfort. The Sir Samuel Mico Trust is still active in Weymouth.

"To-night came in the Mary of Weymouth from Virginia, homeward bound today..." Charles II State Calendar, 1676

Charles II's reign lasted from 1660 to 1685. Besides the religious schisms of the time, his rule was also marked by the return of the plague, the Great Fire of London, the second and third Anglo-Dutch wars, and of course, the ever-increasing taxes to rebuild the capitol and to fight those wars.

❈ ❈ ❈

In the 1660s, the plague returned to British shores. London was the hardest hit, but it also made its way to Dorset. Although it had appeared sporadically after the first major epidemic in the 14th century which began in Melcombe Regis, the 17th century scourge was the worst since that time. There was little written about the plague's impact locally, but harbour towns were always more vulnerable to diseases than other communities because they were ports-of-call for sailors from all over the world. That is no doubt why Weymouth suffered from outbreaks of the plague in 1604, 1607, 1624 and 1625. The only record of deaths comes from the 1607 outbreak, when 37 victims were buried in the cemetery of Radipole's church and six in the Melcombe common. In the 1666 outbreak, there was little impact locally, but the neighbouring towns of Sherborne and Poole were much harder hit, losing a large percentage of their populations. Typhoid arrived in Weymouth in 1691 on a French ship, but the death toll was not recorded.

✽✽✽

Charles II was keen to leave his mark on the country, and he achieved that through some very impressive building projects. In an odd way, his efforts were assisted by the 1666 Great Fire of London, when much of the capital city went up in flames, burning down important buildings like Whitehall and especially important to local history, St. Paul's Cathedral. Enter architect Christopher Wren.

Hauling Portland Stone

WEYMOUTH ET MELCOMB REGIS

One of the most famous architects in British history, Christopher Wren was familiar with Inigo Jones' earlier refurbishment and additions to St. Paul's. After the Great Fire, Wren was chosen to redesign and supervise the rebuilding of the church. Part of that supervision included trips to Portland to oversee the quarrying and shipping of the massive stones the church was going to be made from.

The first problem Wren encountered was with the pier that had been built for the earlier restoration of the cathedral under Inigo Jones. It had been destroyed by a landslip in 1665. Without it, there was no way to load the stones onto the ships which had to take them along the Dorset coast and up the Thames River. In 1675, the king ordered the pier to be rebuilt. At the same time, improvements like replacement of the old quarry equipment that was no longer adequate were made and the road work necessary to help with movement of the stone and equipment was completed.

Did the king take an interest?

In the Weymouth town charters, a single line noted "The King seems to have been lately in the Borough, the Corporation borrowing £100 to meet the cost of his reception."

Sadly, during Charles II's visit in 1673 a fire swept through the town, the second in 20 years. The king must have witnessed what happened and granted Weymouth leaders £3000 - about £250,000 today - to rebuild. This helped to employ craftsmen who repaired and replaced burned down homes and businesses, many of which had had thatched roofs.

Trouble on Portland

Wren visited Weymouth and Portland regularly to identify the best stone for St. Paul's and to try to keep the peace with the quarrymen and his overseers. It was at this point, because the Crown quarries alone could not provide enough stone, that Charles II gave his permission to open up the common lands traditionally farmed by Portlanders to quarrying. The islanders were not granted any compensation for the destruction of their farms, which left many bitter and angry, a situation that paved the way for problems between Wren and his assistants and the local people for years to come.

By 1678, feelings were running high between Wren's site manager, Thomas Knight, and the Portland quarrymen. Knight was a poor supervisor and owed the men back wages. In anger and frustration, they gathered together to demonstrate their frustrations, rioting and destroying quarrying equipment as they went. The king considered their actions so serious, he told the rioters to choose representatives from the group to speak on their behalf. Those men met with the monarch himself in London.

The only thing that came out of the extraordinary gathering was an apology from the men and the promise that there would be no more disruption to stone production, which was slowing down the king's rebuilding projects.

Portland Quarrymen

Wren's work resumed after the quarrymen returned, but the cathedral was not completed until well into Queen Anne's reign. And the animosity between Wren the architect and the Portland quarrymen continued to the bitter end, demonstrated in a letter he wrote to the leaders of that group:

12 May, 1705…*Gentlemen, I have perused yours of the 9th to myself and Mr. Bateman, and find you'll never make a right use of any kindness for which reason you may expect less of mine for the future. You have been paid hitherto beforehand, but without your better behaviour, you shall not be paid so again, though you may always depend on what is right. I shall not add to my last direction about the money, till that be fully complied with, nor at present tell you the price charged to the Duke of Buckingham. As for the stone sent to Greenwich, I know no risk you have run, nor of any proposed to you; so that you have no pretence to higher pay, on that account. 'Tis all one to me what your jury do. It shall not alter any measures of mine, except in endeavouring that the*

tunnage money you claim by a pretended grant from the Crown, be disposed to better purpose than you apply it to, you having no manner of right to it, as I shall easily make appear, and also represent to the Queen your contesting her right, and your contempt of her authority; for, though 'tis in your power to be as ungrateful as you will, yet you must not think that your insolence will be always borne with, and though you will not be sensible of the advantage you receive by the present working of the quarries, yet, if they were taken from you, I believe you might find the want of them in very little time ; and you may be sure that care will be taken both to maintain theQueen's right, and that such only be employed in the quarries as will work regularly and quietly, and submit to proper and reasonable directions, which I leave you to consider of, and am Your friend, Chr. Wren. P.S. — I am sorry Mr. Wood has paid you the tunnage money, but if I have not a better account of your behaviour, I shall endevour that you be made to refund it; and whether your jury present Mr. Wood or not for the stone, 'tis all one to me. If you take upon you to pay the duty for any stone, for St. Paul's or other uses that I give orders for, you shall not have one farthing allowed you for it.

What was it like to be a Portlander

A description of Portland life during the Wren era provides an insight into what must have been quite an isolated place: "All natives of the Island are free both sons and daughters, and the daughters have this privilege that if one of them marry an alien, and have for her dowry a paddock (or little inclosure) by vertue thereof she invests her husband with the freedom of the quarry, and from that time he is admitted free. Every pad-dock is divisible into as many parts or shares as the owner pleases, and each part has an equal title to the quarrys with the whole. An instance may explain this: A has an inheritance of an acre and has four daughters to bestow it upon. He divides it by partition-walls into four parts and gives each of them a part. The conveyance is in this manner. After Evening service on a Sunday when the churchwardens and some of the best inhabitants are placed in the church porch he stands up and expresses himself to this effect: *'I, A, desire you my neighbours to take notice, that I give to each of my daughters an equal share of my paddock called and bounded &c. as it now lies divided in four parts. Whereupon the assembly rises, and blesses by name the daughters. And now each of these daughters intitles the man she marrys to all the Privileges of the King's quarrys, which renders her a good fortune to a mason many whereof go from London and marry thus in Portland.'"*

St. George's church was built on Portland out of Portland stone in the 1750 - 60s and was designed by local mason Thomas Gilbert who was inspired by Christopher Wren's work.

The practice of dividing land amongst both daughters and sons was called "Gavelkind," a tradition inherited from the Anglo-Saxons. The disadvantage of the practice was that it continued to break up tracts of land, which after generations, meant smaller and smaller holdings, which in turn encouraged men, especially, to leave the island in search of work. The practice

Portland's St. George's Church

did not end until just before WWII.

The Second Anglo Dutch War

Like his father before him, Charles II found himself embroiled in conflicts with Holland, known as the second and third Anglo-Dutch Wars. These extended conflicts were fought between 1664 to 1667 and 1672 to 1674. On the eve of the second war, local coastal defences were again in poor condition, with very little money dedicated to their upkeep or the personnel to man them.

The reason or part of it was because Charles Stewart, the Duke of Richmond and lord lieutenant of Dorset, and one of the king's right hand men, had tried to usurp the authority of the lieutenant-governor of Portland and captain of Sandsfoot Castle, Humphrey Weld. At the beginning of the second Anglo-Dutch war in 1664, worried inhabitants of Wyke Regis, all too aware of the poor state of their castle, petitioned Weld to help stop the planned removal of the few troops stationed there. They had heard a rumour that this was part of the duke's plan for reorganising the defences of the county. Given that traditionally, Wyke tenants had provided some of the men on watch at the castle, as well as their food and other provisions, they were exempt from paying crown taxes for that purpose, which did not help their case.

The castle needed a lot of repairs and because the crown was looking for ways to fund the war effort, it did not want to have to pay for that work. Making it worse, Richmond apparently felt that the castle was not even worth saving because, to his mind, it did not provide sufficient protection to make renovation a worthwhile expense. The two sides were at an impasse.

A similar arrangement existed for Portland, where the inhabitants supported forty soldiers who were supervised by the lieutenant-governor of the Isle. Portlanders also asked Weld to prevent the loss of their defences, but he was powerless to stop Richmond's alterations and was dismissed from the lieutenancy for his opposition.

Sandsfoot Castle

Although Weld and the people of Wyke eventually got their own way, Sandsfoot remained open and occupied by the local militia, both Wyke and Portland were forced to continue to contribute to the county militia on top of paying new crown taxes, which, Weld claimed, was contrary to the express orders of the king.

The fear of war, the anger over taxation, and the possible loss of coastal defences, left local people very angry, so much so that a committee was created to try to solve the problems. It was made up of representatives of the king, along with the Earls of Bath and Anglesey. In 1665, those men came up with a compromise. They wanted Sandsfoot castle demolished, but also recommended restoration of Weld's lord lieutenancy and jurisdiction over

Portland.

Even with the restoration of Weld, Portlanders were still paying county rates in September 1665, when they petitioned the crown to end them. The following month Dorset coastal defences were still being demolished in spite of the new taxes, and it appears that even with the new monies paid to the crown, locals were not getting value for their money. By the summer of 1666, a correspondent to the king wrote about how vulnerable this coast really was: "*Weymouth and Portland are unable to make any resistance if an enemy should come...all the sea coast is without arms and ammunition, though before these late times every county had a magazine and noblemen and gentlemen arms and horses ...*"

It was only after the Dutch navy's raid on the English fleet at Chatham in the summer of 1667, where much of the English force was destroyed with little effort, that a programme of coastal and hinterland defensive works was undertaken. The raid made it obvious how vulnerable much of the coast was to attacks. Even then, progress was slow.

Catholic Weld - Years later, Humphrey Weld was in trouble again. He was accused of plotting rebellion against the king. In 1679, at the advice of the Lords' Committee for investigating 'matters relating to the late horrid conspiracy,' he was deprived of the governorship of Portland Castle and his commission of the peace, and the Privy Council directed that Lulworth Castle, which belonged to Weld, his home in Portland Castle and 'Weld House' in London, 'should be searched for arms.' The problem was not that anyone really believed Weld was conspiring against the king, he had simply made some powerful enemies while trying to protect the interests of local people.

In Weymouth, progress was hindered by the lack of leadership; no one seemed to be able to direct the process. The officer in charge of improvements, for instance, did not receive written orders from the lord-lieutenant concerning the fortifications. He did not want to go ahead with building without those instructions for fear of being prosecuted by landowners for damaging their lands by putting up new defensive walls and other structures. There was even a shortage of building clay in the town. Then there were the money problems.

Supplies had to be brought in from other parts of the country, but the borough treasurer was pleading poverty and refused to contribute. Money also proved to be a big problem with the coastal garrisons throughout the spring of 1667; many of them were not properly armed and militiamen either deserted or fell sick because of the lack of provisions.

On and off throughout the 1660s and 70s, there were efforts to both reorganise the defences of Dorset and its militias, as well as to collect the king's taxes. None of these efforts were terribly successful and the local defences were never really properly armed or manned during that time.

Wyke's contribution - The 1670 Weymouth town charter records the local contribution to defence at Sandsfoot Castle: "Imperfect Receipt by Major Bury, Muster Master, for £6, money paid for 'the Militia of this Towne,' by the Mayor, etc. With Seal of Arms and another with a cypher. Oct. 20, 1670. Also £2 paid Sept. 25, 1671." That amount equates to £664 in today's money, still not a lot for the security of an entire village.

The Royal Navy...

The diaries of Samuel Pepys, a Member of Parliament and prolific writer of the time, recorded Weymouth's part in the Dutch-Anglo wars, to include a little-known local cottage industry.

Towns like Chatham and Portsmouth are included in most histories of the Royal Navy not just for their harbours and docks, but because they had industrial-sized mills that produced the cloth and the sails for naval ships. But as the navy grew, the manufacture of those important goods was not limited to the bigger ports, nor was it always done on a mass scale. The sail cloth and cordage made in Weymouth, as well as other parts of Dorset, for instance, were not made on a grand scale, rather by 'poore men, that cannot for beare theire moneys, but must be payd on delivery.' That is how Pepys' friend and informant, a naval captain based in Weymouth who was responsible for the payment and delivery of the sailcloth, described the local sail cloth makers.

The local weavers worked on looms and other equipment in their own homes, demonstrated by the letters sent from the captain to Pepys, who was interested in the sail makers because of his position in the navy office in London. The weavers of Weymouth were independent of the naval administration and the captain complained that unless he could get cash to pay them, they would sell their cloth, as they had done before, to private persons in Bristol, for use on merchant ships. The Weymouth weavers may have been poor, but they knew something about getting the most for their goods.

The illegitimate son…

Charles II and his wife never had children together, but in 1649 he did have an illegitimate son by his mistress while he was in exile in Holland. In 1662, two years after Charles was restored to the throne, he brought his son, James Crofts, to court and a year later, made him the Duke of Monmouth and then, the Captain-General of the Armed Forces. By 1674, James was a powerful man at court and was married to the wealthy Countess of Buccleuch, Anne Scott.

In 1680, James travelled around the West Country, visiting Dorset and winning the approval of many locals. In fact, there was a growing movement to assure the king's illegitimate son inherit the throne when Charles died. One of James' biggest supporters was a Dorset man, Lord Shaftsbury.

He was concerned about Charles' brother becoming king, preferring the king's son. Dorset was, after all, one of those counties that had suffered terrible religious persecution under the Catholic-sympathizing Charles and Monmouth was a Protestant. That was not the plan, however; Charles II wanted his younger brother, James, the Duke of York, to inherit the throne.

Although the Duke of Monmouth had nothing to do with it, he lost favour with his father when the Rye House Plot was hatched by Monmouth supporters in 1683. Their intention was to kill both the King and his brother to ensure the succession of Monmouth, but the plot was a complete failure and because of his father's ill feelings toward him due to the conspiracy, Monmouth took himself off to Holland where he lived as a voluntary exile. He was still there in 1685, the year his father died and the Duke of York became King James II.

"A Monmouth, A Monmouth, the Protestant religion," cried the people of Lyme...

Rather than stay away from England, or make peace with his uncle and settle down to a quiet life at one of his or his wife's estates, Monmouth was convinced by his supporters in England, Scotland and Holland, that he was the rightful heir to the English throne and had such a huge following that he could dethrone his uncle. At their urging, four months after his father's death, Monmouth landed with his volunteer forces at the Cobb in Lyme Regis, beginning his bid for the throne in Dorset. The people who witnessed the arrival of Monmouth's three ships ran to shore and greeted him with the same excitement he would receive throughout the county.

Local recruits joined the Duke as he marched through the county, but they were met early on by the King's forces, led by Commander John Churchill, the son of Winston Churchill, squire of Minterne Magna. The forces clashed at Bridport, but Churchill's men forced the Monmouth volunteers toward Somerset. Monmouth escaped, travelling past Weymouth, hoping to escape on a ship from Poole. He was captured, however, and executed in London the following week.

"The attested copy (dated Jan. 9, 1685) states that the prisoners were put on board the Happy Keturue, at Weymouth, in Portland Road, ROGER WADHAM Commander, &c. They were delivered to Mr. JOHN BROWNE and Company, Factors for Sir WILLIAM BOOTH, Knt., at the Barbadoes. From "The original lists of persons of quality… political rebels…, 1600 – 1700"

James II did not forget the local rebels, however, and a judge famous for his incredibly cruel sentences was appointed to hear their cases at the Court of Assizes. Jeffreys began his search for Monmouth's supporters in Winchester, finally ending up in Dorchester. The legal hearings were dubbed the "Bloody Assizes," because his punishments of the men, and one woman, were so brutal. Of the men tried at Dorchester, 238 were shipped off as slave labour to plantations in the West Indies and Virginia, leaving on two ships from Weymouth. The rest were sentenced to death.

"1 head at the Grand Piere. at Waymouth Towuend. 1 head neere the Windmill. at Waymouth Towneball. 2 heads at the Bridge. 2 heads at Melcomb Towneball"

Judge Jeffries ordered the Dorset sheriff, William Lewes, to build a gallows for the Weymouth executions along the boundary of Melcombe Regis and Radipole. The men were beheaded and their bodies drawn and quartered, then boiled; the pieces - heads, torsos, legs - were displayed on poles. Weymouth's poles were placed on the pier, in the centre of town, on the Esplanade, in front of the town hall, and on the town bridge. Surrounding communities were also the recipients of the gruesome reminders not to cross the king: Preston, Radipole, Upwey, Wyke Regis, Bincombe and Sutton Poyntz all received body parts with orders to display them.

By virtue of an Order to the Sheriff, W. Lewes, from "the Right Hon. Lord Jeffery," and a Precept fromtlie Sheriff to the Mayor, etc., commanding them to erect within the Borough "a sufficient gallowes for the executing the several persons sentenced and appointed to be executed on Tuesday next within your said Borough," it is ordered that the Gallows be erected on or near Greenhill in the confines of the Borough. " Twelve persons being executed . . . their heads and quarters were disposed of by the Maior according to the Sheriff's pcept...as followeth ," Oct. 14, 1685. To Bill of Disburstm for y" Gallows,Burning & Boyling y" Rebells executed, pord" att this Towne £15, 14, 3 Costs.

To add insult to injury, the crown did not even cover the costs of all this. Weymouth town leaders had to pay 'for the gallows, burning and boiling the rebels executed at this Town.' The cost added up to almost sixteen pounds, approximately £2,400 in today's money.

Humiliation as punishment

Judge Jeffries was not satisfied with just transporting and executing the rebels; as those men were led to their final ends, they were whipped as they walked through their towns and villages. One of them was a young Weymouth boy. William Wiseman, a fourteen-year-old barber's assistant, had been asked by rebels of the town to read the proclamation of Monmouth, announcing the intention of the king's son to take the crown by force. The rebels were illiterate and Wiseman could read. For his crime, he was ordered by Jeffries to be walked through Dorchester, whipped by a sheriff as he went. The sheriff went easy on the boy, but a Church of England priest yelled at the sheriff for not striking him hard enough. When Jeffries found out, he ordered William marched through Weymouth and Melcombe, whipped so severely that he fell ill and died of that illness before any other punishments could be carried out.

One of Portland's Lighthouses

MALVASIA

Although ale had always been the drink of the poor and working classes and the addition of hops to the brewing process in the 1600s made much tastier varieties, the consumption of wine really spiked in the 17th century. By 1677, Joseph Williamson, an influential English government bureaucrat who followed the trends of the time, noted that: "As to our necessary dependence on the Spanish in our trade they in some parts depend more on us, as in the Canaries, all that wine being solely brought into England. So that the Islanders would rebel, should Spain interdict the English that trade." He was referring to the new passion for a variety of wine grown and distilled in the Canary Islands – Malvasia. The English called it Malmsey.

By 1681, London customs officers taxed enough Canary wine to fill roughly 4.5 million quart bottles. But it was not just Londoners who loved the stuff. By the 1690s, people all over the country, especially along the coasts, were drinking it in huge quantities. In 1691, the residents of Weymouth and Portland clustered along the harbour, panicked by the horrible sight of what they thought was the return of the Spanish armada. It turned out that this flotilla of hundreds of Spanish ships was the "Canary fleet," loaded with Spanish wine making its way to Dorset harbours.

By what warrant...

Local leaders had a shock in 1687 when James brought a Quo Warranto - meaning "by what warrant" - against Weymouth and Melcombe Regis. This had been done under Charles I too, but neither king's efforts had come to anything. When a regent called for a Quo Warranto against a town, it was out of concern that the community had become too powerful, requiring the regent to step in and replace local power with his or her own. Elizabeth I had given the towns the right to elect four members of parliament, which meant that at that time, with the exception of London, it was the only single borough to have that right. Apparently James II felt a community that could send four MPs to London was a threat to his power.

Fortunately, either because his reign was both tumultuous and brief or because the town clerk sent to London to plead for the dropping of the Quo Warranto was very persuasive, nothing came of the threat to remove Weymouth's unique status.

James' rule only lasted from 1685 to 1688, and it was anything but peaceful, even with the Monmouth Rebellion quashed. He was a practicing Catholic and did not believe in freedom of religion, which meant the persecution of many Protestants while he was king, as well as general upheaval because of the lingering question as to James' legitimacy as heir to the throne. Locally, the impact of the king's cruel treatment of the Dorset Monmouth rebels combined with the birth of a son in 1688 by the Catholic queen, led the leaders of those who wanted James off the throne to ask his

Protestant son-in-law, Dutch king William of Orange, who was married to James' daughter Mary, to bring his army to England in order to help expel James and to take the throne himself.

The Glorious Revolution

There was strong support locally for this choice of leadership; John Digby of Sherborne Castle signed the petition to bring William to England. When the Dutch king arrived, he headed straight for Dorset, to Sherborne, where he issued a proclamation telling the English people that he had come to liberate them, not to conquer them. At that point, James' army, under the leadership of John Churchill, went over to William's side. The king fled in fear for his life, and Parliament invited William and Mary to become joint constitutional monarchs. The Glorious Revolution began in 1688 and was over in 1689, with little loss of life.

With the advent of William and Mary's rule, English monarchs' power was formally limited and Parliament became a full partner in all matters of state. But that does not mean Britain was a democracy.

The Slave Trade

As the New World expanded, the desire for a bigger and bigger work force meant that the process of indenture, which had been the backbone of the plantation expansion that had been feeding the European love of sugar, rum, molasses and tobacco since the early 17th century, was no longer sufficient to support the growth of those trades. Enter African slavery.

Throughout the 17th and into the 18th centuries, all the ports of Dorset were involved, especially Poole, Weymouth and Lyme Regis, where slave ships left to cross the Atlantic. They were loaded with locally made goods the plantation owners ordered from Dorset merchants, picked up slaves in Africa, and delivered their cargoes to the West Indies.

Although the English were not the only slave traders, and buyers, in Europe, they were a significant part of the business. According to some historians, by 1778, the entire English countryside was littered with estates built with the profits from the slave trade. When Prime Minister William Pitt estimated the 1798 income tax from just the West Indies alone, it came to four million pounds.

There were wealthy Dorset families who made their fortunes as plantation owners. Some of those brought slaves home to work on their English estates. Locals who benefitted from the trade often drove in carriages so opulent, the story goes that on a visit to Weymouth, King George III and Pitt encountered a wealthy sugar plantation owner newly arrived home from Jamaica. His staff wore livery and his carriage was much grander than the king's, which led a disgruntled George to say: "Sugar, sugar, eh? All that sugar! How are the duties, eh, Pitt, how are the duties?" The King may not have liked being outshone by a plantation owner, but he did like the taxes the trade brought to his coffers.

But there were also local people who hated the institution of slavery; Weymouth and its neighbours had their own abolitionists. Methodist preacher John Wesley published his "Thoughts Upon Slavery" in 1774; this was a catalyst in informing the British about just how Africans were captured and transported and moved many nonconformists, especially Quakers, to join the anti-slavery movement.

Then there was labour and slavery reformer Thomas Fowell Buxton, who arrived in Weymouth in the early 1800s, winning a local seat in Parliament in 1818, where he worked to banish slavery in England, as well as pushing hard for prison reform. Buxton's brother-in-law, William Forster, moved to Dorset and became another influential local abolitionist. Rear-Admiral William Allen, born in Weymouth in 1792, was also a committed abolitionist and worked to continue the fight to end all slavery, not just English. He wrote books about the subject and travelled on naval expeditions to Africa to help stop the trade.

A change in harbour fortunes…

By the turn of the 18th century, the British were continuing their pursuit of empire, which meant bigger and better ships were needed to make that happen. But there was no renaissance of naval activity in the local harbours. The primary reason for the lack of interest in Weymouth's harbour was twofold. First, the ships of the 18th century were bigger than those of previous centuries, which meant they were in greater danger if they hugged the rugged coast line. They also needed larger and deeper ports than Dorset had to offer.

Making things worse, by the late 17th century Weymouth's quays and other facilities were not well-cared for, which meant the harbour began to silt up, making it dangerously shallow. This became such a problem, by 1708 the Newfoundland fishing fleet, which had been based primarily in Weymouth, deserted the town for the port of Poole, a move the residents of that Dorset town ended up regretting. It made the fleet and its sailors that much more vulnerable to the French, who took full advantage of the easy target at various times later in the century.

> Kearsley's Traveller's Entertaining Guide Through Great Britain (1803): Weymouth, Dorset. Its port is injured by the sand; from which circumstance and the rise of Pool, its trade which was once considerable, is now reduced.

The lack of shipping activity was so acute, the same year Weymouth town leaders called for assistance from the royal customs to help with repair of the quays, piers and the town bridge, but especially the harbour which was 'choked up with sand occasioned by the ruins of the said quays and bridge.' It was so bad that only small ships could navigate it, as compared to those of up to 300 tonnes in years before.

The poor condition of the harbour was matched by lack of

maintenance of the coastal defences, a problem that became apparent when concerns over renewed attention the area was getting from pirates meant local people were once again looking for ways to protect themselves. A three-year survey, from 1714 to 1717, documented just how bad things were.

Although that survey did take note of the importance of Portland castle's role in saving ships from being attacked and or stolen by "privateers," by 1717, Sandsfoot castle was down from twenty-one guns to three, and that was not strictly accurate given two of those were on the beach below the castle and the other was a rusted hulk. Worse, the local government's decision to allow the town to tear down many of the walls of the fortress to repair the town bridge was not really a complete building anymore.

Elsewhere, in Melcombe, there were four guns in the blockhouse, eight in the Mountjoy battery, and two at the jetty, but the guns at Weymouth's Nothe were no longer functional and on Portland, which had had considerable defences only a few decades before, there were no guns left at all.

Pyrates, Corsairs, Buchaneers, or Privateers

They come very often in gangs of sixty to one hundred men to the shore in disguise armed with swords, pistols, blunderbusses, carbines and quarterstaffs...

Pirates were certainly not a new sight for the locals, but the 18th and 19th centuries saw a renewed surge of French, Spanish and Corsair ships along the Dorset coast. As the decades passed, laws and the financial interests that were dictating what was happening on the world's seas, meant piracy just became more organised and sinister. This did not mean, however, that *privateering*, that slightly more "legitimate" form of piracy, had ended. There were many captains carrying letters of marque giving them official sanction to steal in the name of the English regent; in fact, the 18th century was the heyday of that kind of piracy.

It was so lucrative that there were syndicates formed of not just noblemen and country gentlemen pooling their resources to buy and arm merchantmen, but 'bakers, bankers, butchers, cheesemongers...grocers...

invested in commerce-raiding activity.' The hope of catching enemy ships loaded with valuable goods went beyond these private attempts, though. Many naval officers made their fortunes from mixing military duties with more private pursuits.

Jane Austen's *Persuasion*, which takes place in part in Dorset, and mentions Weymouth, demonstrates how some lucky naval officers benefitted from the practice. Spinster Anne Elliot turned the young Captain Frederick Wentworth down when he asked her to marry him. Her family disapproved of her marrying a man without wealth. The heartbroken captain went back to sea and made his fortune plundering Spanish ships; he returned with a fortune, 2.5 million pounds in today's money. The story reflects the reality of the time, when this kind of privateering made many English naval officers wealthy; the English navy was not shy about using the possibility of wealth as a recruitment tool.

Austen's opinion of Weymouth was not terribly high. When she wrote to her sister after what must have been a holiday in the town, she said: 'Weymouth is altogether a shocking place I perceive without recommendation of any kind and worthy only of being frequented by the inhabitants of Gloucester...'

Tolerated in smuggling

The 1717 to 1719 records of customs collector Phillip Taylor of Weymouth tell the story of just how much smuggler activity there was in the local communities; he reported on the "the running of great quantities of goods having of late very much increased." Reports like these led to pressure on parliament to pass a bill that would make smuggling illegal, but the House of Lords refused to pass it. Literate smugglers took this as a sign that the government approved of their "work" because they were *tolerated in smuggling by the King, Lords and Commons.'* This did not help customs officials whose job it was to collect those taxes and prosecute people who did not pay them. More from Phillip Taylor's reports:

"…the smuggling trade is prodigiously increased and they and all persons concerned with them are become more insolent than ever and dares any power to oppose them, which will very soon have a very bad influence on trade. Besides, as these smugglers are generally the dissatisfied part of the country, their riding in troops of thirty or forty armed men on the least appearance of an opportunity will be dangerous to the peace of the country as well as troublesome to the Government."

A reluctant House or not, the problem was so extreme, the public call for legislation continued and a bill to prevent smuggling finally passed a year later. It stated that no ship under fifty tonnes could work in the importation business, but according to the same customs collector, it did not stop the local smugglers as 'the tumultuous and riotous proceedings of the smugglers is not anything abated but daily growing upon us…The smuggling traders in these parts are grown to such a head that they bid defiance to all law and government. They come very often in gangs of sixty to one hundred men to the shore in disguise armed with swords, pistols, blunderbusses, carbines and quarterstaffs; and not only carry off the goods they land in defiance of officers, but beat, knock down and abuse whoever they meet in their way; so that travelling by night near the coast, and the peace of the country, are become very precarious; and if an effectual law be not speedily passed, nothing but a military force can support the officers in the discharge of duties.'

Although the new law allowed local authorities to hang anyone found guilty of smuggling, the customs collector wrote not of the fear the law created, but the power of the men involved with the "trade": *'Most of the smuggling trade in this country is now carried on by people in such great numbers, armed and disguised, that the officers, if they meet them, can't possibly oppose them therein, nor do otherwise than search for the goods in suspected places, which by means of the country's favouring the smugglers, very often proves ineffectual and expensive to the officers.'* A big part of the problem of course was that so many "respectable" citizens were involved.

"at Dorchester fair"...

In spite of the efforts of Lewis and other officers of the law to end smuggling, it is probable that 1719 was one of the most profitable years ever. Two runs on the Dorset coast, one at Worbarrow Bay, the other at Bridport, had at least five boats unloading goods, described by an observer at the time as 'a perfect fair at the waterside, some buying of goods and others loading of horses; that there was an army of people, armed and in disguise, as many in number as he thought might be usually at Dorchester fair, and that all the officers in the county were not sufficient to oppose them.' In Bridport, the specialty was brandy and salt brought to shore and 'carried off by great numbers of the country people.' The customs officers just stood there, watching all the activity, outnumbered by the smugglers and their customers.

That same year, customs officers from Weymouth raided Lulworth Castle and the surrounding area, knowing that its owners the Weld family, like so many other well-to-do citizens, had links to the trade and allowed goods to be stored there. The maids helped by using candles in the windows to warn smugglers when there were customs officers on sight or were expected. It was reported that the groups of men coming and going from Lulworth often comprised up to 100, all armed and ready for a fight. They knew every nook and cranny of the hills and inlets of the entire area, storing their ill-gotten goods to assure the king's men could not find the casks, barrels and trunks.

Smugglers in Lulworth Cove

Sowing the crop...

Like centuries before, wine and brandy continued to make up a large part of the smuggled goods arriving in Weymouth and surrounds on English and foreign ships, but there were other items that sold very well, including silks and other cloth, paper, salt, tea, playing cards and goods that reflected the growing market for more exotic food and drink like pepper, cocoa beans, coffee and rum.

Before the law and subsequent supporting laws were passed to try to end smuggling, both pirate and smuggler ships had anchored close to the shores, often just beyond Weymouth harbour. They waited there while crews of men could be rounded up to collect the goods. Another act was passed in 1719 to stop ships from anchoring up to six miles off the coast - without official permission - which was supposed to help stop this loitering. Instead, canny smugglers used the excellent hiding places they and others before them had established near Osmington at Upton Mills, at Tyneham village's tiny Warbarrow Beach, and at Lulworth Cove. They would stash their booty in caves, accomplices' homes, and they even floated large casks of alcohol in the sea. These were held down by weighted ropes until the heavy containers could be collected safely. This practice was known as "sowing the crop."

Osmington Bay

Of course, sometimes "sowing" did not quite work out as planned. A group of local fishermen from Abbotsbury came across an unusual "catch" in November 1720, off of Burton Bradstock's shore. They found 25 barrels of brandy and wine "moored with ropes to stone." The find, oddly, ended up starting a fight amongst local gentry and officers of the law that went all the way to London.

Thornhill's St. Mary's Church

The fishermen pulled the casks to Abbotsbury, where they handed them over to the village excise officer, a Mr. Whitteridge. Then they were taken, presumably by force, by the bailiff of Thomas Strangways, the Earl of Ilchester. That bailiff, a William Bradford, declared that his employer was entitled to the "find" because of his position. Weymouth custom's official Philip Taylor did not agree and ordered his minion, young customs officer based in Abbotsbury, to get the casks back. That officer, a Joseph Hardy, did just that, only to have them taken away again by a group of hostile locals, possibly on the order of the Earl's bailiff. Taylor was not impressed when he commented upon Whitteridge and Hardy's capabilities: *'They being both the most original fools I ever met with or heard of, in the scuffle of taking the goods away I can't find any blow was struck on either side and (it appears) that the heroical officers were directly frighted out of their goods.'*

Portrait of a Portraitist - As smuggling reached its peak, a new Member of Parliament for Weymouth was elected in 1722. Although he did not appear to make much a name for himself as a parliamentarian, James Thornhill did make a name for himself as an important 18th century artist. Born in 1675 at the White Hart Inn in Melcombe Regis to the daughter of Colonel William Sydenham, governor of Weymouth, Mary Sydenham, and Wareham grocer Walter Thornhill, he was appointed the Court Painter by George I in 1718 and knighted in 1720. His paintings could be found in St. Paul's Cathedral, Chatsworth House, Blenheim Palace, Hampton Court, the Chapel of All Souls College at Oxford University, as well as Weymouth's St. Mary's Church. He was also a portraitist whose subjects included Sir Isaac Newton. Thornhill began his own art school and his most famous student was William Hogarth, who married the MP's daughter Jane in 1729. When Thornhill left Parliament in 1734, his voting record did not indicate he had spent a lot of time representing issues important to the locals, spending most of his time in London, living at Covent Garden, but he certainly put Dorset on the map as far as important 18th century artists were concerned.

The tale went on. Taylor knew most Abbotsbury residents were employed by the Earl, so he decided to call in the army, which led to the bailiff changing his mind and giving up the alcohol. His boss, however, did not drop the matter and complained to the Secretary of War, claiming he was owed the casks because they were salvage, not smuggled goods. If that had been true, calling the army in to deal with the matter was an infringement of his rights. The matter seems to have ended there; Strangways did continue to lobby members of parliament he knew to take up his cause, but nothing came of it.

Abbotsbury's Strangways Hall

Back at the Crown Inn

Going back to the 13th century, during and after the reign of Edward III, Osmington Mills had been an important location as far as smuggling was concerned. That had not changed into the 18th century, thanks in part to a cartel of families who had lived there for generations. Enter Emmanuel Charles.

Emmanuel was born into one of those smuggling families in the 1780s. Besides trading in smuggled goods, many of which he sold at his pub the Crown Inn, Emmanuel and the rest of the Charles family and their relatives owned and operated smuggling ships, to include The Integrity, a somewhat ironic name for a smuggler's boat. They used this to carry goods on runs between Lulworth Cove and Weymouth.

These local men offer a glimpse into the violent world of the smuggler; Emmanuel's son Richard was caught by local *Preventer* men (agents of the regent who were supposed to find and arrest smugglers) while he was running a load of smuggled goods. When he resisted, they shot him and he died of his injuries. His uncle spent a lot of time in gaol because of his violence during smuggling operations, and a cousin died during a fight on board the family ship, when he was tossed overboard and drowned. And the "profession" and its inherent violence meant that the following generations of Charles, though they remained smugglers, were in constant turmoil, with at least twenty-seven serving time as convicted criminals.

In spite of that, Emmanuel Charles managed to become quite wealthy. He ended up living in Radipole, where he built a fine home known as Radipole House, right on the water's edge, although it appears he actually died quite a poor man; his brother also lived in Radipole and eventually became an innkeeper. In subsequent generations, the family retired from smuggling and were legitimate local business people.

Honesty in their heart…

Although not unique to Portland, the islanders were especially adept at not just smuggling, but its cousin, *wrecking*. This practice had been around for hundreds of years, but it was such a problem by the 18th century, a law against it passed in 1752. This law piggybacked another law passed the year before which raised taxes on alcohol, a move calculated to limit the lower classes' drinking, but with the unintended consequence of increasing smuggling and wrecking. Neither had any impact on local wrecking.

William and Mary

The Glorious Revolution was a bloodless one, and meant that the former enemy nations were now allied. This alliance had its benefits, but it also brought the British into the next European conflict, the Nine Years War, which was fought between various European powers, roughly allied into two camps: William led one of them, the king of France the other.

Although a very complex conflict, fought mostly on European soil, its impact was felt on the Dorset coast when the French fleet was sighted off

Weymouth and Melcombe Regis in 1710

of Portland bill in June of 1690. This terrified the Weymouth population who thought that the French were there to invade. Fortunately, the English-Dutch fleet was in hot pursuit and the two navies fought a major battle further up the coast, a battle that left the French untouched, but with a loss of eleven ships for the English-Dutch.

The sighting of the huge French fleet led to yet another call for better protection for the local communities, but by1694 little had been done and Weymouth trade had been badly affected, as its primary trade partner was France, which was now its enemy. That meant that the French had control over the English Channel throughout the war, cutting Dorset ports off from their traditional export-import outlets.

With the renewed threat to the British coast, the navy went through another period of growth and with the demand for more and more ships, Weymouth was considered as a location for a new ship yard, but because during low tide the water level could be dangerously low, the decision was 'to add no more precludes entirely.' In other words, it lost out on that opportunity.

Lighting the Coast

Lighthouses - structures built to contain large fires meant to illuminate hilly areas or dangerous outcroppings - were placed around the English coast by the Romans, locations that may even have been used by earlier people for the same purpose. The construction of a modern system of lighthouses around the British coast, however, did not begin until the 17th century (in East Anglia), spreading quickly as canny businessmen saw the potential for profit in building and maintaining them at public expense. But the agency responsible for granting permission for the structures, the Trinity House Corporation, did not feel a lighthouse was necessary when a Cornwall speculator, Sir John Coryton, applied for permission to build the first lighthouse at Portland Bill. That was in May 1664. It seems, however, their refusal was more about politics than an honest belief that there was no need to have a lighthouse on the Bill. It was and still is one of the most dangerous places to navigate in the UK, with five different currents meeting and where many ships over the centuries have met their ends.

A second try also failed when Captain William Holman of Weymouth, supported by local ship owners and the Corporation of Weymouth, petitioned Trinity House again, only to be told there was no reason to build an expensive lighthouse on the Bill. Finally in 1716 another petition on behalf of the people of Weymouth was accepted and King George I gave permission for the first local lighthouse, with a sixty-one year lease to a private consortium to build it. But the building was not well-maintained and the fires that acted as the light source often went unlit, proved by a 1752 inspection by Trinity House officials who reported 'it was nigh two hours after sunset before any light appeared in either of the lighthouses.'

Finally in 1789, William Johns, a Weymouth builder under contract to Trinity House, took down one of the towers and erected a new one at a cost of £2,000 (£170,000 today); this was lit by a large oil lamp rather than an open fire. It had been re-sited to assure that ships could navigate their way through to the Channel or Portland Roads.

Concerns over navigation in the 18th century also led to a growing use of lightships, boats permanently anchored, with powerful oil lamps attached.

The other Portland Lighthouse

Portland Lighthouse, 1790

Weymouth Harbour from Wyke Regis

WHAT A CENTURY

Rocked by international wars, aggressive Imperialism, and the beginning of the industrial revolution, the 18th century saw dozens of conflicts throughout Europe and beyond, some spreading to the New World. The French and English clashed in Quebec, which led to Canada being claimed as an English colony, the American colonies broke away to become an independent nation, and the East India Company and the British army fought the local powers in parts of India, paving the way for the British Empire's control over that part of Asia.

The War of the Spanish Succession, the Nine Years War and the Seven Years War saw the English military engaged in many corners of the globe. Although the days of heavy recruitment in the port towns of Dorset were over, there were still many men from the local community serving their king - or queen - and country, all over the world, to include the Dorsets, whose proper name was the Dorset Regiment, formed in the 17th century and still serving today. Local men in the regiment in the 1700s found themselves in the Netherlands, Spain, France, Portugal and North America.

"Blow wind, rise sea, ship' shore' fore day!" *The call of the Portland wrecker*

Like earlier wreckers, those active in the 1700s kept watch for any boat running along the isle's shores that appeared to be, or clearly was, in trouble. One of many memorable incidents took place in 1762 when a Cornish vessel loaded with casks of wine broke up on Chesil Beach in a winter storm, its cargo washed into the sea. Portland and Weymouth citizens rushed to grab all the wine they could before the customs house officers arrived. In the end, the locals managed to salvage twenty-six casks that night, and another ten the next day. The officers only managed to find ten.

The following year, 1763, a French man-of-war, the *Zenobie*, was also wrecked on Chesil. Although the crew managed to save themselves, the locals, looking for something to take away with them robbed and stripped the men; the survivors were championed by the king, who ordered the provision of clothing and transport back to France. In other incidents involving native and foreign crews and passengers of ships unlucky enough to get into trouble along the coast, the wreckers' victims were not so lucky.

> *Not sever'd from the shore, aloft where Chesill lifts*
> *Her ridged snake-like sands, in wrecks and smouldering drifts*
> *Which by the South raged, are heaved on little hills...*
> *Which running on the Isle of Portland pointeth out...*
> "Polyolbion" by Drayton

Possibly the most dramatic of the recorded wrecker incidents of the 18th century occurred in November 1795 when a 200-ship strong English naval fleet made up of men-of-war, West Indiamen and transport ships led by Rear-Admiral Hugh Christian, left from Jersey, carrying 16,000 soldiers, dozens of merchants and their families and the ships' crew, all of whom were headed to the West Indies. When the weather turned foul as they sailed toward the Dorset coast, some of the ships broke off and made it safely to Torbay and Portsmouth, but others stayed on course along the Chesil, where they 'thunder with resistless violence against that fatal bank, of stones, which beginning at the village of Chisle, on the…Isle of Portland,' scattering crews and soldiers as they did so. Instead of helping the victims, though, locals, mostly Portlanders, headed to the shore looking for booty.

The death toll that day was over 1,600 and the actions of the locals was not lost on onlookers, especially the person who recorded the incident. Those first Portlanders 'who are always praying for wrecks on their coast and whose whole attention was devoted to plunder' were joined by 'a considerable mob from different parts solely intent on plunder,' until the local military arrived, shooting into the crowd to break up the scene.

Honesty in their hearts…

In a sermon by the Reverend Thomas Francklyn from the tiny church in Fleet, he preached against wrecking after he had witnessed an incident in 1754 where wreckers had taken over a ship, tossed its crew overboard, and stolen its cargo. He lamented over how often he had 'tried to stir up principles of compassion as well as honesty in their hearts.' The good reverend also reminded his parishioners of the fact that parliament had just passed a law making wrecking punishable by hanging, but the wreckers knew they outnumbered the local constabulary and king's agents.

Lower inhabitants of this coast

There was even a book written about one of the many 18th century wrecking incidents. This exert demonstrates what it would have been like to go through such an ordeal: *'Mr. Darley escaped by throwing himself from the wreck, at a moment when she drifted high on the stones: he reached them without broken limbs, but the furious sea overtook him, and carried him back, not, however, so far but that he regained the ground; and notwithstanding the weight of his clothes, and his exhausted state, he reached the top of the bank, but there the power of farther exertion failed him, and he fell. While he lay in this situation, trying to recover breath and strength a great many people from the neighbouring villages passed him - they had crossed the Fleet water in the hopes of sharing what the lower inhabitants of this coast are too much accustomed to consider as their right, the plunder of the ships wrecked on their shore and, in the gratification of their avarice, they are too apt to forget humanity. Scenes like these call forth the most honourable, and discover the most degrading qualities of the human heart. Mr. Darley seems to have been so far from meeting with immediate assistance among here who were plundering the dead, without thinking of the living,*

(otherwise than to make some advantage of them also) that though he saw many boats passing and repassing the fleet water, he found great difficulty in procuring a passage over for himself and two or three of his fellow sufferers, who had by this time joined him: having, however, at length passed it, he soon met with Mr Bryer, Surgeon of Weymouth, to whose active humanity all the unhappy sufferers were greatly indebted; on his reaching Weymouth, the gentlemen of the South Gloucester sent him every supply of necessaries that his situation required - and all the soldiers and sailors were taken care of by Mr. Warne, Agent to the Commissioners for the Sick and Hurt.' From "The Loss of the Catharine, Venus, Piedmont, Thomas, Golden Grove and Ælous, 1795, on the Chesil Beach Industry in the 18th century"

❊ ❊ ❊

Although there had been silk mills in Dorset for hundreds of years, it was in the second decade of the 1700s that silk manufacturing began to rival the wool industry as a vital part of the Dorset economy. This shire was one of the five that were now known internationally for their excellent cloth. Thousands of local people were employed in the industry, to include throwsters (workers who twisted the silk threads), spinners, winders and dyers. Villages like Cerne Abbas were hives of silk weaving activity, along with other local villages and towns. Once the silk had been woven and was ready for sale, it was sold to buyers who then sent it on to merchants, both by ship and overland.

It was not too long, however, before the industry experienced one crisis after another. When the Industrial Revolution kicked off in the 1760s, one of the first major innovations it introduced was the water frame, an automated way to spin cloth. Up to this point, all cloth was made on hand looms, usually in the homes of the spinners. The water frame required investment in purpose-built buildings dedicated to weaving, and those had to be next to freely running water, both of which meant workers had to go to the industry as paid labourers instead of having a measure of control over the production and delivery of the product.

With this shift came a depression in wages, something that was made more acute by the new importation of cheaper silks from other countries. It became such a problem that silk workers were one step from starvation for decades, leading them to send representatives to the House of Commons, in an attempt to make their plight known at the national level. Amongst other things, they hoped that Parliament would vote to end the importation of the foreign silks.

Adding to all these difficulties, the silk industry found itself challenged by a fairly new trade, one that many skilled silk workers deserted their industry to join, and whose English roots were also found in Dorset.

The Dorset Button

Before the 15th century, clothes were held together with ties. Then Europeans began using buttons and button holes to keep garments together, something they were likely to have been exposed to through trade with Asia where the practice was thousands of years old. Sometime after the late 1500s, there were a handful of local women who began making buttons at home, but it was an English soldier who while serving in France saw how the skilled button workers there made the little device on a larger scale. He brought the techniques home with him.

When Abraham Case left the military and settled in Shaftsbury, he opened his own *buttony* business, employing individuals to make buttons that he could sell to merchants and the tailoring trade. This was in the early 17th century. Over the years, the demand for buttons grew and grew, making buttony a very important industry, one focused in Dorset. In the 18th century, it employed thousands of women and children and was worth at least £12,000 pounds (£900,000 today) a year. The centres of the home-based industry were Blandford, Bere Regis, Lytchett Minster, Langton Matravers and Poole, but there were also individual workers producing in Weymouth, Wyke, Portland and other villages and surrounding farms.

Dorset's position as the country's leader in button making was also helped by the fact that wool was manufactured locally and the two industries worked hand-in-hand; the bases of the buttons were formed out of discs taken from the horns of Portland sheep. Wool made from those sheep provided the backing for each button, meaning buttony and sheep farming worked hand-in-hand, from Portland to Shaftsbury.

There were two types of buttons made in Dorset, high tops and knobs, both covered with linen, which provided a base for the fine thread that was used to embroider the designs unique to each type of button. Within those too broad categories of button, there were numerous styles, some with interesting

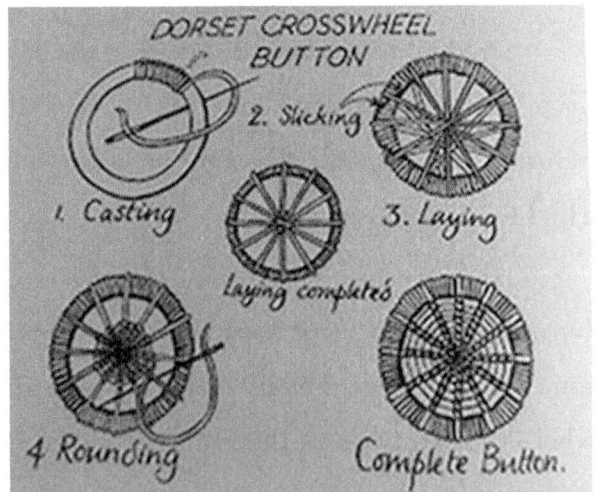

Dorset Buttons

names: Blandford Cartwheels, Spangles, Birds Eyes, Ten-Spoke Yareels, Basket Weavers, Gems, Mites, Cross Wheel of Spiders Webs and

Honeycombs.

The Buttoners

Although bending over tiny buttons many hours a day would not have been easy, the women who chose to work in buttony were better off than they would have been working in the fields, labour that was driven by the seasons and the weather and that paid very poorly. The average woman field hand, one of the few 'professions' open to women, could make only a small percentage of what the buttoner could earn. Really skilled master buttoners could earn up to three shillings, nine pence (£16 today) for a package of 144 buttons, the prices depending on the quality.

By the 1740s, the business had expanded so much "depots" were set up around the area, where button workers went to sell or trade their buttons to the Case company's representatives. Those were in Lytchett Minster, Milbourne Stines, Sixpenny Handley, Piddletrenthide, Langton and Wool.

In to the 19th century, the industry was doing so well, several schools dedicated to teaching girls how to make buttons were set up in Bere Regis, but buttony met the same fate, though much later, as the silk industry when button making machines replaced buttoners. Whole families of button makers became destitute. Those who could, approximately1,000 of them, emigrated to America, Australia and Canada, most leaving on locally owned ships from Weymouth harbour. Many of the local buttoners who could not emigrate, especially the widows who were completely reliant on button making, ended up in the Wyke, Weymouth and Melcombe Regis, along with other, workhouses.

Parliament's button - A beneficiary of the Case family tried to revive the button industry in the early 20th century by specialising in making coloured buttons for Dorset members of Parliament, but the attempt to expand ended with the beginning of WWI.

I saw thee first (full forty years ago) On coach-box mounted,
reins and whip in hand,
Guiding thy nags, with steady pace and slow,
On Weymouth's pleasant, health-inspiring strand...

The Hanoverians and Georgian Weymouth

A new royal line emerged in the 18th century, beginning with German-born King George I, who spoke little English and visited London from Germany only when he absolutely had to. He was followed by his German-born son, George II, who also preferred to live in Germany, though he did learn to speak English. With so little time spent in the kingdom they were ruling, it is little wonder that there was no royal presence, or interference, in the local communities during their reigns. That changed in quite a dramatic fashion when George III, the son of George II, took the throne. He was the first Hanoverian king born in England and he lived in London for most of his life. It was this King George who helped bring Weymouth back into the national spotlight.

The Sea washes away all the Evils of Mankind. Dr. Richard Russell, 1750

The 18th century history of Weymouth and its neighbours is a chequered one: with a silted up harbour, its life as an important port of call was not what it had once been. Now it was more famous for smuggling than import-export. But Weymouth's location, with its large sandy beach, a relative rarity in England, along with weather that was far more clement than other parts of the country, brought it another kind of prosperity: tourism.

By the 1740s, doctors and other "health experts" were recommending water as a cure for all kinds of illness as well as a way to maintain health. This was a response, in part, to the terrible outbreaks of the bubonic plague that had continued into that century, along with other horrible contagions that were common throughout Europe. Fear of health problems at least for the middle and upper classes became a bit of an obsession, though bathing at home was at an all-time low amongst wealthy Georgians.

A gentleman who took the health benefits of sea bathing seriously was a Mr. Ralph Allen, esquire, a wealthy resident of Bath in Somerset. In 1750, after discovering the wonders of Weymouth's harbour and he purchased a property on the esplanade. Allen had reformed the ancient British postal system, which had made him a very rich man; he invested his fortune in quarries near Bath, England's most famous spa town. Georgian Bath was built from the stone Allen quarried. As he was a wealthy and famous man, he attracted wealthy friends, to include the Duke of York, who visited him in Weymouth in 1758 to do a bit of sea bathing himself.

Allen even commissioned a bathing machine for this own personal use, though he was not the first to use one of those portable changing rooms. As early as September 1748, two men were granted twenty-one year leases to build and place two wooden bathing houses on the Melcombe Regis side of the harbour; by 1780, there may have been as many as thirty of the contraptions scattered along the seafront, all available for a day's hire.

The booming 1770s…

Travel to Weymouth became easier in the 1770s when Parliament, in 1771, passed an act to fund a turnpike road between Dorchester and Weymouth, ending on the sea front. That and the new and very modern bridge linking Weymouth and Melcombe Regis, built in 1770 to replace the old one, continued to make going from one side of the harbour to the other easier, though residents did not like the new bridge, which they replaced again in the 1820s.

Social Weymouth

In response to the growing interest in the Weymouth seafront, another man from Bath, Andrew Sproule, built a new hotel and assembly rooms in 1773. The assembly rooms were a very important meeting place in Weymouth, as they were in other Georgian towns, and the rules for those fortunate enough to afford their use were 'for the preservation of order and decorum; the company are therefore humbly requested to observe the following...' They included: women could not wear riding habits and men were not allowed to wear boots. Neither men nor women were permitted to dance wearing 'coloured gloves,' and men were advised 'That gentlemen will be pleased to leave their swords at the door.'

The Duke

Although Weymouth was experiencing a bathing boom in the second half of the 18th century, it was really in the 1780s, when the town was honoured with a visit from King George III's brother, the Duke of Gloucester, who also found it a pleasing place to bathe and walk, that its popularity exploded. He liked Weymouth so much, he purchased land on the seafront, where he built Gloucester Lodge, which he used as his residence until he sold it in 1791. He lived at Cranborne Lodge in East Dorset making Weymouth convenient for him. It was the Duke who recommended the town to the king, whose health was never very good.

Royal Dippers...

It is thought that George III may have suffered from an inherited ailment called porphyria, a condition of the blood that when really serious, can cause seizures, which he experienced much of his life. One of the "cures" recommended for the illness was sea bathing, something the king did whenever he visited. He came to love Weymouth and Portland so much, he bought Gloucester Lodge from his brother, enlarged and improved it, and it became his favourite place to stay, which he did at least once a year.

Like earlier bathers, George had his own "bathing machine," which

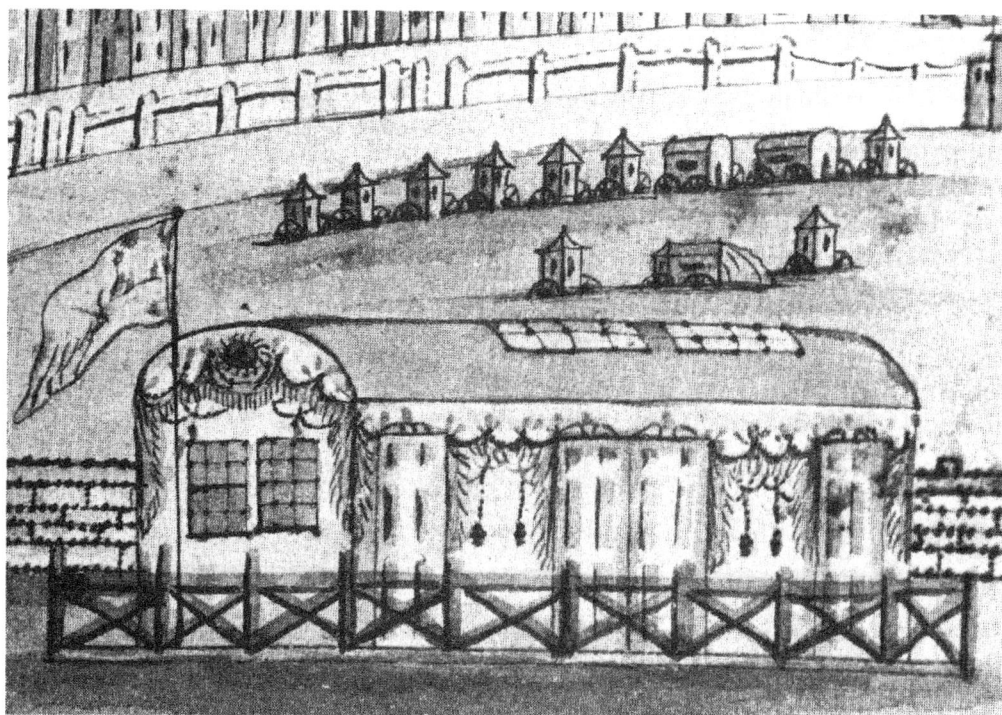

George's Barge

was wheeled down to the water's edge to preserve his modesty; at this point,

Princesses Bathing in the Barge

the bathing costume had not been introduced and it was considered healthful to take a dip in the sea without clothes on. He was lowered into the water by the "royal dippers" and when the king came out of the water, a band played "God Save the King."

When George realised he was going to be a regular visitor to Weymouth, besides his bathing machine he had a large floating "barge" built that created a sort of sea pool, with grills that allowed water inside, and included 'modesty hoods' which could be pulled down over the steps the bather used to get into the sea. It was intended to provide the ultimate privacy for the king and his family, but it must have been quite humid and airless.

> The Wishing Well – The village of Upwey, which means the upper part of the River Wey, has a natural spring, which is the source of the river itself. Going back thousands of years, residents have believed the spring has magical health benefits. George III and many of the wealthy tourists who visited the Weymouth area agreed. Whenever he was staying at his lodge, he would ride to Upwey to drink the waters.

It was George's new passion for sea bathing at Weymouth that not only put the town on the national map, it made it a truly fashionable place to visit. Wealthy people flocked to the town, which in turn meant a huge increase in property prices - 500% - and a major building boom, which is why the sea front today is dominated by Georgian buildings.

> St. Nicholas Church- The 14th century church at Broadwey was partly damaged in a 17th century fire, but much of the ancient structure was saved when it was repaired later in the century. This is where George III and his family worshiped on Sunday's, probably before his visits to Upwey, which was another mile up the turnpike.

Civic Pride

Many of the town improvements of the late 18th century were based on the king's keen interest in the community. By the early 1780s, there were so many wealthy visitors to the town that a "Road Bill" was introduced into Parliament in April of 1782:

George III's Weymouth

Weymouth, &c. Road Bill.

Message was brought from the House of Commons, by Mr. Ewer and others: With a Bill, intituled, "An Act to enlarge the Term and Powers of an Act made in the First Year of the Reign of His present Majesty for repairing and widening several Roads leading to and through the Towns of Weymouth and Melcombe Regis and Dorchester, in the County of Dorset; and for repairing the Road leading from the Parish of Warmwell through the Parishes of Poxwell and Osmington to the Church in the said Parish of Osmington, in the said County of Dorset;" to which they desire the Concurrence of this House.

There were numerous mentions of the road in the Parliamentary records of that year, to include the statement that the bill had been passed:

Weymouth, &c. Road Bill

Hodie 3ᵃ vice lecta est Billa, intituled, "An Act to enlarge the Term and Powers of an Act, made in the First Year of the Reign of His present Majesty, for repairing and widening several Roads leading to and through the Towns of Weymouth and Melcombe Regis and Dorchester, in the County of Dorset; and for repairing the Road leading from *the Parish of Warmwell, through the Parishes of Poxwell and Osmington, to the Church in the said Parish of Osmington, in the said County of Dorset." The Question was put, "Whether this Bill shall pass?" It was resolved in the Affirmative.*

Civic Improvements

Local leaders wanted to continue to attract more visitors and through another act of Parliament were allowed to tax local businesses to raise the money to make Weymouth an even more appealing town. There were street lights installed along the newly paved roads and night watchmen were employed to help control crime, which in turn meant visitors would feel safe when they went out, especially at night, which was good for business. Footpaths were also improved and kept clean, helped by a local ordinance that prevented people from riding their horses or driving cattle on the town's footpaths.

Many of the improvements of the late 18th century may have been intended to continue to make Weymouth an attractive tourist destination, but they would have had some benefit to the broader community. Fire was a problem throughout Dorset because of the thatched roofs so popular for thousands of years. A law was passed in an attempt to stop this problem by requiring, in 1794, all new buildings have slate, tile or lead roofs. Melcombe Regis also established a fire department, complete with piped water and a twelve-man crew of fire fighters

To keep the peace as well as keep town traffic moving, there were also steep fines levied on anyone who blocked traffic unnecessarily. And Weymouth was one of the earliest towns to establish a public lending library, called "J. Love's Circulating Library."

Pennsylvania Castle and the Royal Yachts

The Penns return

The Penn family had had a connection to the local area going back to the Dutch-English Wars, and that history was revived with the arrival of George III and his wife Queen Charlotte. One of her ladies-in-waiting was none other than the wife of William Penn, the son of William Penn, the founder of Pennsylvania. Juliana Fermor Penn travelled to Weymouth with the royal entourage, accompanied at times by her son, John, who loved the area, especially Portland, as much as George did.

It was during one of the royal visits when the king and John were given an extensive tour of Portland and John was introduced to Church Ope Cove, with its spectacular views of the English Channel. The king owned the land and he agreed to sell it to the younger Penn.

Because of John Penn's royal connections, he was able to hire the man often referred to as George III's architect, James Wyatt, to design a Gothic revival "castle" near this beautiful spot. Penn was given the governorship of Portland, a position that gave him even more valuable land on the Isle, and his was and remains the grandest building ever built there. It was especially poignant for the residents of the island to see such an elegant mansion being built out of the stone they had quarried. Though for centuries many of the grandest and most famous buildings in England had been built out of their stone, few locals would ever have seen them.

...there is no want of any Thing, that is necessary for the Maintenance and Support of Man; since both Sea and Land seem to vie with each other, and strive which shall indulge his Appetite most, and yield the greatest Abundance. To All this we must add, that its fine Beer and Ale are universally admired, and by some preferred before the Wines of France. And as its abounds thus with Provisions of all sorts, which are to be procured likewise at very reasonable Rates, it is no great Wonder, that such a Number of Families, even of high Distinction, make it their favourite Place of Abode.
From "The Natural History of Dorsetshire, 1757"

Because of the natural springs found in the Weymouth area and its surrounds, it has been possible to brew beer since at least the time of the Celts. Most of it was home brewed for family consumption or for barter. The process was so important, by the 16th century even some of the smallest Dorset villages had their own malt houses and all of the market towns had at least one. This is where the malt, that key ingredient in beer, was prepared in larger quantities than was possible in the home by part time *maltsters* who sold the prepared malt to home brewers. An excellent example of a malt house serving a busy village was Abbotsbury's, probably built by a member of the Strangways family in the 16th century.

From the Middle Ages, public houses and inns brewed their own beer for sale, but even those had to buy their malt from the malt houses. The first brewery in Weymouth, where beer has been brewed professionally since at least the 13th century, was located in what is now called Brewer's Quay. There was a free running spring near by (river water was rarely used in beer brewing, because rivers, to include the Wey, were handy for the disposal of town sewage) and the barley grown in the fields behind Radipole supplied the grain.

Abbotsbury malt house

When hops began to be used, those had to be brought in from further afield, often Kent. Local maltsters supplied the malt until the 19th century, when both processes were combined, which also signalled the decline of home brewing. Until the 1750s, about sixty-percent of all beer brewed was still made for personal consumption; by the end of that century, Dorset had numerous breweries leading to a drastic drop in home brewing. Weymouth, Dorchester, Poole, Blandford, Cerne Abbas and Bridport, to name a few, all had bustling breweries. They offered a boost to local economies by employing maltsters, drivers, bottlers, clerks, coopers, and many more. Some even had their own rat catchers! Beer remained an important staple in the Dorset diet well into the 20th century.

Lulworth Village

When Irish playwright John O'Keefe visited Dorset, he enjoyed not only the people, who were the inspiration for his play "The London Hermit: or rambles in Dorsetshire," a three part comedy which takes place in Dorset, he was also very impressed with the wonderful food he enjoyed. He even left a written record of a lunch he had at an inn in West Lulworth. The menu, which included chicken, lamb, fresh produce, and gooseberry pie with thick cream, all washed down with home brewed ale, was one of the best he had ever eaten. He was just as complimentary of his suppers which included crab and lobster, along with cucumbers, cold lamb, butter and bread and his breakfasts of: "Suchong tea, sugar, honey, cream, milk, home-made bread, and rolls, butter and eggs." Having lived in London for many years, he was genuinely surprised at the freshness and quality of the Dorset-grown meals.

The playwright was in good company, even George III, when he visited Weymouth and Portland, ate local food, which he loved, rather than the much fancier fare that most monarchs indulged in. He and Queen Charlotte were known to prefer plainer foods, so much so that the pundits of the times lampooned them for it, but George clearly enjoyed local cuisine. He looked forward especially to meals at the Portland Arms, where he ate his share of the pudding that was the landlady's specialty, along with Portland lamb and mutton, and a local baked good called a Radipole biscuit. But what did the *average* person eat?

The Portland Arms

his frugal GRACE –
The Mail arrives! Hard! Hard! The cheerful horn,
To MAJESTY announcing oil and corn;
Turnips and cabbages, and soup and candles;
And lo, each article GREAT CAESAR handles!
Bread, cheese, salt, catchup, vinegar and mustard,
Small beer and bacon, apple-pie and custard;
All, all from WINDSOR greets his frugal GRACE,
For WEYMOUTH is a d-mn'd expensive place.
From the satirical poem "The Royal Tour and Weymouth Amusements" by
John Wolcot in 1795.)

Portland Washerwomen

BULLOCK'S CHEEK

Although boosted by tourism - and wealthy tourists ate well - the local economy of the 18th century was not a rich one. Those who lived outside of the town were mostly rural labourers and small farmers who raised sheep for the wool industry, hemp and flax for the rope industry, cows for butter and cheese and barley for the production of beer. Over 60% of the population was working poor. In fact, as the century was coming to a close, rural Dorset was one of the poorest areas in England, the result of a complex historical mix of public grazing land being enclosed by the gentry, growing mechanisation of farming, and a growing population, all of which shaped the dramatic economic and social problems of the 19th century.

Even when staples like corn were fetching high prices, those who worked the land as paid labourers could barely afford to eat, let alone eat well. When the prominent social reformer of the late 18th century, Sir Frederick Eden, travelled around the country to find out about the living conditions of the working classes, he was shocked at what he found in Dorset. He described the inadequate weekly diet of a local Dorset family:

> *The usual breakfast of the family is tea, or bread and cheese, their dinner and supper, bread and cheese, or potatoes sometimes mashed with fat taken from broth, and sometimes salt alone. Bullock's cheek is generally bought every week to make broth. Treacle is used to sweeten tea instead of sugar.*

Scurvy grass...

Just like centuries past, locals gathered plants that grew wild along the shoreline, things like sea kale, samphire, and berries. There was never a shortage of watercress in the rivers and in the nearby countryside, there were plenty of rabbits, though as the 18th century progressed, more and more of what had once been public land that anyone could hunt or gather from was being enclosed by wealthy land owners, in some cases making access to free food a potential crime. But locally, fish and shell fish were abundant, especially for the people of communities like Weymouth, Portland and their seaside neighbours.

A local recipe book written in the 1760s included recipes made from local ingredients, many costing little or nothing: boiled carp, crab, herring, and sprats, watercress soup, rabbit pie, mutton casserole, jugged hare, and lots of stodgy puddings were cheap and filling. The book included a recipe demonstrating an understanding of the medicinal benefits of some of the free greens found locally. It explained how to make a healthy drink from watercress and a coastal plant called scurvy grass. What the writer had come up with – or inherited – was a drink that provided an excellent source of nutrients, specifically vitamin C, which prevented a common problem for sailors and others with a limited diet: scurvy. This may have been why the key ingredient was called scurvy grass.

Portland Fishermen

The inevitable consequence of poverty is dependance...Samuel Johnson, 18th century writer

As demonstrated by the plight of the silk workers, the latter half of the 18th century saw the beginning of the industrial revolution and with that, the beginnings of the displacement of traditional workers. The same thing was happening with farm workers and other labourers, who increasingly found their meagre wages eaten up by a sharp increase in food prices, something that began in Dorset in the 1750s, and spiked in the 1780s.

Sir Eden wrote about the plight of the Dorset labourer in the 1780s: *'The rapid rise of the poor rate in this parish is generally attributed to the high price of provisions, the smallness of wages and the consolidation of small farms and the consequent depopulation of villages which obliges small farmers to turn labourers or servants.*[1]

Similar to the Tudor era, when Parliament began to tell communities how to deal with their poor, by the middle of the 18th century, poverty was once again a political issue. This was due, in part, to the fact that as the number of needy grew, so did local taxes paid to support them. In response to the complaints they received, Parliamentarians commissioned a study in 1777 to find out just what was happening around the country with the management of poor relief; the report found that there were 1,916 workhouses in England, with an average of 90,000 paupers living in them. That did not take into account those who received "outdoor relief" which was the payment to the poor who remained in their own homes or were vagrants.

Locally, there were at least 28 community facilities, which included: Burton Bradstock with 12 inmates, Charminster with 20, Dorchester with 80, Fordington with 20, Lytchett Minster with 15, Melcombe Regis with 44, "St James in the Town and County of the Town of Pool" with 80, Portesham with 50, and Wyke Regis with 20. There were others, like Melcombe Regis, but their inmate numbers were not noted. The need for so many facilities, which were miserable places to live, says something about how difficult life was for many locals. In fact not long after the turn of the 19th century, 15% of the local population was receiving poor relief.

The treatment of those who were forced to live in the towns' and villages' workhouses was harsh and remained so well into the 20th century. Able bodied men and women were expected to work for a minimum of eleven hours a day; the men performed heavy labour in public gardens and for community businesses, some working in the quarries; the women were required to clean, take care of the resident children, and some who were considered fit were put to work on looms, to include being trained to make the local specialty - bone lace - a design brought from the Netherlands and made by Dorset weavers since the 1690s. No one, no matter what duties they carried out, received any wages. Even children were expected to perform manual labour as well as to attend workhouse schools. If overseers considered the behaviour or actions of inmates unacceptable, they had complete power over them; they could be locked up against their will, starved into submission or physically punished.

Although the exact locations of some of the workhouses is unknown, it is assumed that all or most of them were located in the same places as their 19th century replacements, when a need for ever-more places for a growing number of poor meant the demand for larger facilities. It is certain that Melcombe's was near the Quay and Weymouth's was on the site of the still-standing 19th century facility on Wyke Road.

Where ever they were placed, the late 18th century workhouse demonstrates the darker side of life at that time in history. And the turn of the 19th century would, in many ways, bring even greater challenges to the local people. Enter Napoleonic Wars.

The Next Chapter…

By the turn of the 19th century, Great Britain was changing at a manic pace, but nothing had as dramatic effect on that era as the Napoleonic Wars, which began in 1803 when the British declared war on the new French emperor, Napoleon Bonaparte. The second volume of the story of Weymouth, *From Napoleon to Nuclear Submarines* will begin with the impact those wars had on the local community, and continue through to the on-going Enclosure Movement, poor reform, the Industrial Revolution, the return of the British navy, Dorset's literary boom, the impact of two world wars, and so much more about the place and its people.

Waters Edge, Portland

AUTHOR'S NOTES

The research for this project has been thorough and like all histories, there is always more to say. Sources from which I have built the story of Weymouth and its neighbours include but are not limited to: Historical Archaeology, Journal of Roman Studies, Architecture & Architectural History, English Historical Review, Journal of British Studies, Albion: A Quarterly Journal Concerned with British Studies, English Historical Review, Britannia, Classical Philology, Cambridge Historical Journal, Economic History Review, Transactions of the American Philosophical Society, Memorials of the Counties of England, Economic History Review, Transactions of the Royal Historical Society, Oxford Journal of Archaeology, and Journal of International Peace Operations.

Other vital sources include muster, pipe and tax rolls, minutes from royal societies and community councils, royal charters, private letters, works of literature, works of art, account books, and early antiquarians' accounts of their own and earlier eras. Biographies have been useful, as have church records, old newspapers and even cookbooks have been examined for clues to the lives of those who came before us.

Volume II, **From Napoleon to the Nuclear Submarine**, will continue this story, picking up where Volume I ends, with the Napoleonic Wars. That series of conflicts had a profound impact on all of Europe, to include individual communities. Dorset was no exception. The research for that book, which is currently on going, will be no less diligent.

INDEX